CO-AUV-905

Volume X
Publication No. 106
November 1980

Divorce,
Child Custody
and the Family

Formulated by the
Committee on the Family
Group for the Advancement of Psychiatry

MENTAL HEALTH MATERIALS CENTER

30 East 29th Street, New York, N.Y. 10016

Library of Congress Cataloging in Publication Data

Group for the Advancement of Psychiatry. Committee on the Family. Divorce, child custody, and the family.

(Publication—Group for the Advancement of Psychiatry; v. 10, no. 106) 1. Divorce—United States. 2. Custody of children—United States. 3. Children of divorced parents—United States. I. Title. II. Series: Group for the Advancement of Psychiatry. Publication—Group for the Advancement of Psychiatry; no. 106.
HQ834.G77   1980   306.8 '9   80-25935
ISBN 0-910958-10-6

Printed in the United States of America

TABLE OF CONTENTS

TABLE OF CONTENTS (cont.)

TABLE OF CONTENTS (cont.)

This is the seventh publication and the last in a series of publications comprising Volume X. For a list of other GAP publications on topics of current interest, please see last page of this publication.

STATEMENT OF PURPOSE

THE GROUP FOR THE ADVANCEMENT OF PSYCHIATRY has a membership of approximately 300 psychiatrists, most of whom are organized in the form of a number of working committees. These committees direct their efforts toward the study of various aspects of psychiatry and the application of this knowledge to the fields of mental health and human relations.

Collaboration with specialists in other disciplines has been and is one of GAP's working principles. Since the formation of GAP in 1946 its members have worked closely with such other specialists as anthropologists, biologists, economists, statisticians, educators, lawyers, nurses, psychologists, sociologists, social workers, and experts in mass communication, philosophy, and semantics. GAP envisages a continuing program of work according to the following aims:

1. To collect and appraise significant data in the fields of psychiatry, mental health, and human relations

2. To reevaluate old concepts and to develop and test new ones

3. To apply the knowledge thus obtained for the promotion of mental health and good human relations

GAP is an independent group, and its reports represent the composite findings and opinions of its members only, guided by its many consultants.

DIVORCE, CHILD CUSTODY AND THE FAMILY was formulated by the Committee on the Family which acknowledges on page 792 the participation of others in the preparation of this report. The members of this committee, and the members of the other GAP committees as well as additional membership categories and current and past officers of GAP are listed below:

Stephen B. Shanfield, Tucson, AZ
Mottram P. Torre, New Orleans, LA
Vamik D. Volkan, Charlottesville, VA
Roy M. Whitman, Cincinnati, OH

COMMITTEE ON MEDICAL EDUCATION

Paul Tyler Wilson, Bethesda, MD,
  Chairperson
David R. Hawkins, Chicago, IL
Herbert Pardes, Pomona, MD
Jeanne Spurlock, Washington, DC
Bryce Templeton, Philadelphia, PA
Sidney L. Werkman, Denver, CO
Sherwyn M. Woods, Los Angeles, CA

COMMITTEE ON MENTAL HEALTH SERVICES

Herzl R. Spiro, Milwaukee, WI,
  Chairperson
Allan Beigel, Tucson, AZ
Mary Ann B. Bartusis, Philadelphia, PA
Eugene M. Caffey, Jr., Bowie, MD
Merrill T. Eaton, Omaha, NB
Joseph T. English, New York, NY
Robert S. Garber, Belle Mead, NJ
W. Walter Menninger, Topeka, KS
Jose Maria Santiago, Tucson, AZ
Donald J. Scherl, Boston, MA
George F. Wilson, Belle Mead, NJ
Jack A. Wolford, Pittsburgh, PA

COMMITTEE ON MENTAL RETARDATION

Norman R. Bernstein, Boston, MA,
  Chairperson
Leo Madow, Philadelphia, PA
Betty J. Pfefferbaum, Houston, TX
Carolyn R. Robinowitz, Bethesda, MD
George Tarjan, Los Angeles, CA
Warren T. Vaughan, Jr., Portola Valley, CA
Thomas G. Webster, Washington, DC
Henry H. Work, Washington, DC

COMMITTEE ON PREVENTIVE PSYCHIATRY

Stephen Fleck, New Haven, CT,
  Chairperson
C. Knight Aldrich, Charlottesville, VA

Charles M. Bryant, San Francisco, CA
Jules V. Coleman, New Haven, CT
Frederick Gottlieb, Los Angeles, CA
William H. Hetznecker, Philadelphia, PA
Ruth W. Lidz, Woodbridge, CT
Richard G. Morrill, Boston, MA
Harris B. Peck, New Rochelle, NY

COMMITTEE ON PSYCHIATRY AND COMMUNITY

John J. Schwab, Louisville, KY,
  Chairperson
Lee B. Macht, Cambridge, MA
Herbert C. Modlin, Topeka, KS
John C. Nemiah, Boston, MA
Anthony F. Panzetta, Philadelphia, PA
Alexander S. Rogawski, Los Angeles, CA
John A. Talbott, New York, NY
Charles B. Wilkinson, Kansas City, MO

COMMITTEE ON PSYCHIATRY AND LAW

Seymour Pollack, Los Angeles, CA,
Loren H. Roth, Pittsburgh, PA,
  Co-chairpersons
Edward T. Auer, Philadelphia, PA
Elissa P. Benedek, Ann Arbor, MI
John Donnelly, Hartford, CT
Seymour L. Halleck, Chapel Hill, NC
Carl P. Malmquist, Minneapolis, MN
A. Louis McGarry, Great Neck, NY
Jonas R. Rappeport, Baltimore, MD

COMMITTEE ON PSYCHIATRY AND POLITICS

Paul Chodoff, Washington, DC,
  Chairperson
Viola Bernard, New York, NY
Robert N. Butler, Washington, DC
Jerome Frank, Baltimore, MD
David F. Musto, New Haven, CT
Walter Reich, Rockville, MD

COMMITTEE ON PSYCHIATRY AND RELIGION

Albert J. Lubin, Woodside, CA,
  Chairperson
Sidney S. Furst, Bronx, NY

788

790

Committee Acknowledgments

The Committee wishes to express its appreciation to the many people who have helped in the formulation of this work.

We are most grateful to our legal consultants without whose help this book could never have been written. These include Robert E. Schulman, who began our orientation to the legal issues and Joseph Goldstein, who stimulated us with the provocative ideas of his group. We owe a special debt, however, to Henry H. Foster, Jr., who gradually became our primary legal advisor as he helped us understand, organize and write about the various legal issues.

In addition, we wish to acknowledge our appreciation to Israel Zwerling, a long time member and former chairperson of this Committee, who retired from active membership during the formulation of this work. He helped immeasurably in the early stages by his clear exposition of the family issues.

Also, we wish to acknowledge the contributions of the following Ginsburg Fellows who met with our Committee during the course of our work: Paul J. Barreira, Norman S. Broudy, Karen Hoppenwasser, Leslie L. Morris, Jose Santiago, and Florence M. Young.

We are also grateful to Florence Trefethen who helped edit the first draft of this manuscript and to Eileen Flanagan who typed the final version.

Finally, we wish to express our gratitude to the many GAP members who criticized and made suggestions about the earlier drafts of this report. We deeply appreciate their encouragement and hope we have done justice to their input.

Joseph Satten, *Chairperson*

Divorce, Child Custody and the Family

INTRODUCTION

Family disputes comprise the largest category of civil matters handled by our overburdened legal system. Over half of the cases filed in our trial courts of original jurisdiction are concerned with matrimonial actions, that is, divorce or legal separation;[1] these ordinarily involve issues of child custody and visitation rights. Even where the parents agree on custodial and visitation terms and court approval is routine, changed circumstances may lead to petitions to modify prior custodial orders.[2]

Current statistics show that one out of every three marriages will end in divorce, that this proportion is steadily increasing, and that a majority of these divorces involve children.[3,4] The situation is most serious in California where it is estimated that one out of two marriages will fail and that 70 percent of these will involve children under twelve.[5] As a result, a growing number of children are becoming children of divorce, a fact that has staggering implications for future generations.[6] The determinations of custody for these children are crucial to their development and future mental health.

This report will consider the custody problems of two types of divorces—the "amicable" ones, in which parents are able to come to an agreement about the care and custody of the children, and the contested ones, in which differences are irreconcilable and decisions about child custody have to be made by the courts. Special attention will be focused on current thinking in psychiatry and the potential contribution of mental health professionals to the determination of custody.

In these considerations, the term "custody" has two meanings. The first and traditional meaning is the control of and the right to make decisions about the child, with the recent practice of one parent having primary care and responsibility and the other parent usually having rights of visitation. The second meaning—more important but less obvious—is that of meeting the child's needs, including that of access to both parents. This second meaning is often forgotten because the parents, while fighting each other, tend to see the child's needs as linked to their own individual positions. Moreover, they each have their own advocates, but the child usually has none.

Legal decisions about child custody are the responsibility of the courts, and, through the ages, the legal-judicial system has developed its own principles for deciding about child custody. They are based on centuries of experience in similar situations and on common sense reasoning about human nature. These principles serve as guidelines for decisions when emotion is high and conflicting interests cloud the picture. In discharging its responsibility, however, the legal-judicial system relies not only on these principles, but also on the best available knowledge at any given time.

In this century, the fields of psychiatry, psychology, and the social sciences have developed rapidly. These bodies of knowledge are focused primarily on understanding the life of the individual from birth to death, and the favorable and unfavorable events that influence the course of a life. Some of the building blocks on which many psychological theories rest are findings about emotional forces that may seem to run counter to earlier reasoning about human behavior, for example, the concept of the unconscious. Nevertheless, some of the concepts from psychological and psychiatric theory have gradually been incorporated into the legal principles that govern child custody decisions. To date, the prevailing psychological-psychiatric theory offered to the courts has been based primarily on the study of the individual.

During the past twenty-five years, a new "family" orientation for understanding human adaptation and development has evolved. This view supplements what is known about the life of the individual through a study of the entire family and its multigenerational antecedents. This kind of family orientation, known also as family systems theory, provides important new dimensions for understanding and dealing with problems of coping and adaptation, including those that arise when a family breaks apart.

The emotional processes that result in divorce are set in motion long before the divorce becomes an overt threat or a reality. The family difficulties that lead to divorce are themselves traumatic for all concerned. Decisions about child custody—even without disputes—are among the most difficult of all human decisions. They almost always involve an extensive network of family relationships—old and new. Litigation, especially if bitter and prolonged, can add its own adverse effects to the problems of the family, reaching beyond parents and children to involve grandparents and others in the extended family. And, since the final legal divorce does not end the emotional relationships, these effects may continue far into the future, especially when children are involved.

This report is written for all who become involved with family disruption and divorce where children are affected. It is designed to convey an overall view of the family emotional processes which encompass every member of the family before, during, and after divorce, and which, if understood, can contribute to better decisions about child custody.

Among those most involved in emotional events that lead to divorce and child custody decisions are mental health professionals*—on the one hand—and lawyers, judges, and other personnel connected with family courts—on the other.

---

*We will use the term "mental health professional" to mean anyone trained and working in the field of mental health and illness, most commonly a psychiatrist, clinical psychologist, or a psychiatric social worker.

We believe it is especially important that those working in the mental health and legal professions have some basic understanding as to the other's functions and underlying principles. It is to them primarily that this report is addressed. Specifically, we want to give mental health professionals enough orientation about the legal issues involved so that they can function effectively in this area. Conversely, we want to give lawyers and judges a view of what potentially the mental health field can offer so that an effective involvement is recognized and expected.

Mental health professionals are often the first involved, when the conflict is still contained within the family and before it becomes an adversary process with outside representatives taking sides. In some cases, the couple seeks help for a marital problem and ignores the effects of their differences on the children. In others, a child manifests the problem and is referred for treatment while the conflict between the parents is ignored. In still other cases, the parties involved ignore all but the legal questions; they neither acknowledge nor seek help for any emotional problems connected with the dissolution of the marriage. In all instances where children are involved, however, the effects of marital disharmony on the total family should be considered—before, during, and after the divorce. If the custody problems cannot be resolved, and the case goes on to litigation, we believe that the mental health professional who becomes identified with any one contender in the family conflict tends to become partisan and such an expert is less helpful in the long run than one who thinks in terms of the family as a whole and its needs.

Better understanding of family emotional processes should be helpful to those in the legal field who are involved in child custody decision making, primarily the judges and their ancillary conciliation and probation staffs. We hope this report will also be useful to attorneys who negotiate for and counsel their clients.

This report can help parents who are contemplating divorce or who are actually involved in divorce proceedings. We hope it will further a better understanding of the range of problems involved in child custody decisions as well as encourage all the participants to transcend the narrow and emotional biases that so often prevail at the time of a family's dissolution. The report can also be helpful to teachers, guidance counselors, social workers, and others whose work brings them in contact with the children of divorce. Further, it should give legislators and community leaders a better understanding of the family and thus facilitate more constructive legislation.

Chapter 1 summarizes the breadth and depth of problems that custody determination cases can present and introduces readers to the complexity of the issues involved. In Chapter 2, the historical and legal background of custody cases is described; principles that have been used as court guidelines are examined and current formulations of custody criteria are assessed. Chapter 3 provides an overview of the family-oriented perspective and a brief discussion of recent research on children who are separated from one or both parents. The application of the family perspective to custody determinations is the focus of Chapter 4, which sets forth guidelines on which current decisions should be based. Chapter 5 moves to the stage beyond divorce and to problems that can be addressed in post-divorce counseling. Chapter 6 describes the role of the mental health professional in the legal setting, and Chapter 7 outlines recommendations to the courts to help improve the process of custody determinations.

This report attempts to crystallize what is now known in the area of mental health and apply it to the problem of child custody. Interest is great, and research projects are steadily developing. Before too long, much new data should augment the knowledge now available.

REFERENCES

1. L. M. Friedman and R. V. Percival, A Tale of Two Courts: Litigation in Alameda and San Benito Counties, *Law and Society Review* 10 (1976) 267-301.

2. Michael Wheeler, NO-FAULT DIVORCE (Boston: Beacon Press, 1974) p 72.

3. A. J. Norton and P. C. Glick, Marital Instability: Past, Present, and Future, *Journal of Social Issues* 32,1 (1976) 5-20.

4. R. S. Weiss, "A New Marital Form: The Marriage of Uncertain Duration," in FESTSCHRIFT FOR DAVID REISMAN, H. Gans, N. Glaser, and C. Jenks, eds (Philadelphia: University of Pennsylvania Press, 1978), Chapter 10, pp 221-233.

5. Ciji Ware, Joint Custody: One Way to End the War, *New West* 4,4 (1979) 42-55.

6. Mary Jo Bane, Marital Disruption and the Lives of Children, *Journal of Social Issues* 32,1 (1976) 103-117.

1

DIMENSIONS OF THE PROBLEM

Although the growing incidence and social acceptance of divorce may have resulted in making legal procedures more routine, divorce is no easier emotionally now for the persons involved than it ever was.[1] The process of divorce has a traumatic effect on the entire family, especially the children. The hope that divorcing parents will deal reasonably with each other in matters relating to their children's welfare is often not realized because the partners, however much they have wanted or not wanted the divorce, generally feel hurt, angry, guilty, and inadequate. Even where custodial arrangements are developed through negotiation and compromise, the hurt and guilt that remain often defeat the parents' best intentions.

Fortunately, only 10 percent of the cases go on to full scale legal battles over custody.[2] Those battles, however, have been described by observers at the most bitter and acrimonious they have ever seen in court.[3] Judges almost always try to persuade the divorcing parents to work out a compromise or a negotiated solution, since they, the judges, regard decisions in contested custody cases as most difficult to make.[4]

Custody decisions have become more, not less, complex with time. In the somewhat distant past, when ideas about parental fitness and concepts about child-rearing were more doctrinaire, the father was assumed to be the rightful custodian; more recently it became the mother. In the last decade or two, however, social and legal factors have converged to create a situation in child custody cases in which there are fewer firm guidelines, with the potential for greater conflict over custody and less predictability about the outcome.

Perhaps more important, our society has become more mo-
bile, and families are typically just nuclear families—two parents and their children. The grandparents, aunts, uncles, and
cousins are frequently distant and dispersed. In these instances
there is no extended family matrix in which the nuclear family's problems can be cushioned. There are no nearby collateral
relatives who would, in other times, have played a role in
raising the children. The solution to child custody problems
generally lies increasingly within the nuclear family itself. It
usually involves two angry parents and children who do not
fully understand what is happening.

Further, the trend toward "no fault" divorce—in effect, divorce on the demand of one party, with few questions asked and
few disagreements exposed—screens some of the evidence and
some of the criteria that helped, for better or for worse, to guide
earlier custody determinations. In addition, a "new narcissism," more prevalent in some parts of the country than others,
tends to encourage each partner to "do his or her own thing"
and to put the highest priority upon his or her own personal
fulfillment.[5,6] This has given rise in some cases to a new kind of
custody problem: whereas, formerly, both parents wanted the
children, now there are a noticeable number of divorces in
which nobody really wants the children.[7]

Furthermore, changes in sexual morality and the acceptance
of a wider variety of lifestyles have removed a large body of
criteria on which custody decisions were once based. Finally, a
changing attitude to traditional sex roles, particularly as they
relate to parenting, has resulted in legislation and in court
decisions that there should be "no discrimination with regard
to the sex of the parents" in the awarding of custody. The
decision no longer goes automatically to the mother, although
she remains the favored person unless she is "unfit" or the
father has assumed the child-rearing function.[8]

All these changes complicate the court's deliberation in custody determinations, both in contested cases and in approving arrangements negotiated by the parents. The problems the courts face are difficult and often defy any confidently-expected solutions. Consider, for example, this case in which both divorcing parents want custody and arrive in court after having been unable to work out any compromise solution for the care of their children.

Case 1:

> Dr. C, 32, and his wife, 31, have been married 10 years and have two sons, seven and five years old. Dr. C, a physician, has recently joined an established group practice and is doing well financially. Mrs. C, a nurse by profession, married her husband during his second year in medical school. She helped support him through medical school and early postgraduate training, but quit work when she was six months pregnant with their first child and has not since resumed work.
>
> Their marriage went well at first, but became stormy after the birth of the second child. Mrs. C accuses her husband of being cold, demanding and domineering. Dr. C accuses his wife of being too "wishy-washy" and dependent.
>
> The court gave temporary custody of their sons to Mrs. C. Dr. C feels he cannot accept this arrangement as permanent because he "needs" the children and cannot live without them. He sees his wife as "psychologically unstable," and feels she is "too soft," that she spoils the children and is not ambitious enough for them. In turn, she sees him as immature, extremely self-involved and insensitive to her needs and the needs of the children. She views him as a child who became jealous of her attention to their children.

This not uncommon type of case, poses several problems for the court:

- Can either of these parents be considered "unfit"?

- If neither is unfit, what characteristics of capacities might be considered by the court to be relevant to good parenting?
- What criteria ought to be considered in placing these children, and how might these criteria be weighted?
- Why are the parents unable to negotiate or to reach a compromise? (This is a natural, though perhaps a nonlegal, question. But it may be related to characteristics in one or both parents that are germane to the children's long-range interests.)

The problems cited above increase in number and complexity in many cases of contested custody. Suppose, for example, the wife was in psychiatric treatment, or the husband had been abusive to the wife and children, or either parent had clearly neglected the children. The addition of any one of these factors would make the case more complex, but, at the same time, it would add some specific criteria on which earlier courts have ruled.

Problems also arise when a presumably "settled" custody case is reopened. The courts normally retain continuing jurisdiction over custody settlements and the parties involved may move for a rehearing if they believe "circumstances have changed" in any significant fashion. Here are two cases that demonstrate the emergence of new problems.

Case 2:

Mr. D, 32, and his wife, 30, were married ten years. They have a girl aged nine and a boy aged five. Mr. D is a building contractor. Mrs. D, a junior college graduate, recently completed training as a laboratory technician and has just gotten her first full-time job.

The couple have been separated for eighteen months, during which time Mr. D has lived in the home and has had custody of the children. Mrs. D has visited frequently. The children are doing well in school. They are picked up each afternoon by a high school student, their neighbor, who has been their sitter for a couple of years. She cares for them until about 6:00 p.m. when Mr. D gets home. He then takes over with dinner and the evening arrangements.

Mrs. D, who has completed her training and is newly self-supporting, now wants custody. She feels she would be a better custodial parent than the children's father. She has no special criticism of her husband, but has assumed that she would get custody. She plans to continue similar arrangements for the children in their afternoon hours.

Case 3:

Mr. S, a 26-year-old salesman, and his ex-wife, 23, have been divorced for two years. At the time of the divorce, after a four-year marriage, Mrs. S had felt her home and children were too confining; she wanted to "do her own thing." Mr. S moved toward reconciliation, but his wife felt he was too quiet, too "square." In the divorce settlement, she agreed to let her husband have custody of their son, aged four, and their daughter, aged two. Now, Mrs. S alleges that she "has her act together" and is asking for custody of the children.

After the divorce, Mr. S remained in the home and, with the help of sitters and—later—a girlfriend who moved in, took care of the children. In the first eighteen months after divorce, Mrs. S "ran around" a lot and did not visit the children. In the six months prior to filing her suit, she began visiting them regularly. The visits pleased the children and raised in them the fantasy that their parents might be reunited.

These cases were reopened because of changes in the circumstances on which the initial settlement was based. The usual legal requirement is that there be a "substantial change" in the circumstances.

Cases, however, are reopened for various other reasons. A custodial parent may move to another geographical area or may develop a serious relationship with a member of the same or opposite sex, and the non-custodial parent files for a change. The non-custodial spouse or the parents of the non-custodial spouse may refuse to return the children after a visit, and file for custody instead, alleging the custodial parent is unfit. In all reopened cases, the critical issues for the court involve an evaluation of how the children are faring in their current setting, how they might fare in the alternative setting proposed, and what the short-term and long-term effects of a change might be. These issues are difficult to weigh without input from the children and from mental health professionals.

To illustrate the multiple problems courts face in dealing with custody cases, we trace a fictional case, each segment representing an actual litigated case.

1. Upon divorce, both Fred and Mary request legal custody of their three children—Ann (six months), Betty (thirty months), and Charlie (eight years). Fred is 30; Mary, 28. Mary plans to remain single and to enroll in a school of social work. Fred plans to remarry immediately and to continue to earn his living as a free-lance writer. The marital home will go to the parent who is awarded custody.

Problems:

Which post-divorce household seems to offer more stability for the children? With children this young, particularly the two girls, is the mother the more "natural" candidate for custody? Is it wise to link a financial arrangement such as possession of the marital home to the decision about custody?

2. After the divorce proceedings have commenced, Fred and Mary make an agreement that they will have joint custody and that the children will alternate each week

between the marital home, where Mary will live, and an apartment a block away, where Fred and his new wife plan to live.

Problems:

Is this alternate-week arrangement conducive to the children's immediate security and their long-term development? What does this joint custody agreement really signify in terms of the parents' motives, feelings, and goals? Are the children being given too little consideration or are they being used as pawns in a power struggle?

3. After the court let it be known that it disapproved of joint custody under these circumstances and would not endorse the agreement, Fred proposed that Charlie be placed with him and that Mary keep the girls. Mary had no objection to this arrangement. Fred said that, in such an event, he would move to the suburbs where he had always wanted to live.

Problems:

What are the effects on siblings who are divided between divorcing parents? What new factors enter the case when one part of the sundering family removes itself geographically from the other, reducing possibilities for access among all parties?

4. During the course of the custody proceedings, the judge invited eight-year-old Charlie to his chambers. After offering him some candy, the judge asked, "With whom do you want to live? Which one do you love the most? Which one treats you better?"

Problems:

What weight should the expressed wishes of children
have in custody determinations? At what age ought
such wishes be considered as being reasoned and responsible? How can judges elicit information from
children without giving rise to feelings of helplessness,
guilt, or confusion? What guidelines ought judges to
follow in trying to ascertain a child's preferences?

5. After the court expressed its disapproval of separating
   siblings, Mary let it be known that she and her friend
   Zelda would be prepared to care for all three children in
   the marital home. Fred objected on the grounds that
   Zelda was a homosexual whose affair with Mary had led
   to the break-up of their marriage.

   Problems:

   Is a deviant lifestyle a sign of unfitness in a parent? Do
   unusual family constellations, such as lesbian "marriages," provide inappropriate environments for children, or can children's needs be adequately met in such
   households? What relationship, if any, has homosexuality to the capacity for parenting?

6. Mary conceded that she had a homosexual relationship
   with Zelda. She countered that Fred had a long history
   of mental illness and had spent three months of the past
   year in a mental hospital following a psychotic break.
   When mentally ill, Mary claimed, he was abusive towards her and the children.

   Problems:

   What weight should the mental illness of one parent
   have in decisions involving child custody? How can the
   court evaluate the family's emotional situation, espe-

cially if issues like mental illness are buttressed in court by experts for one or both adversaries? Is a past history of mental illness germane to a present decision about custody?

7. Fred denied that the psychotic break stemmed from mental illness and claimed, instead, that his hospitalization was due to a "bad trip on LSD, which could happen to anybody." He admitted to having once been "hooked" on amphetamines, but stated it was now "over" and that he was "sound as a dollar."

Problems:

Is addiction to drugs a criterion of unfitness in a parent? How ought the court weigh past addiction which has apparently been overcome?

8. Considering Fred as a possible custodial parent, the judge asked him how firm his plans were for remarriage. Under pain of perjury, Fred admitted that, although he had been living with his girlfriend, they had not discussed marriage. His impression was that she preferred the single life. Fred described his girlfriend as an only child who didn't especially care for children, but he thought she would like his kids.

Problems:

What factors ought to be considered in custody cases if a step-parent is part of one or both of the alternative households? What precautions should be generated by a possible "Cinderella factor" in placing children with a step-parent, especially one who "does not care for" children or is deeply involved with his/her own children?

9. The court next indicated dissatisfaction with both Mary and Fred as possible custodians and wondered whether there were grandparents who could serve as a more satisfactory alternative. Mary said her parents were in their forties, but lived 2000 miles away. Fred said that, although his parents lived within 50 miles, they were in their sixties and retired.

Problems:

Under what circumstances ought the court seek someone other than a parent as custodian for the children? If non-parent custodians are sought, how important are such factors as relationship, age, geographical location, etc.? How largely should the children's wishes figure in such determinations?

The case presents a constellation of problems which are magnified far beyond those of a typical child custody case. Yet it by no means exhausts all the possible issues that courts have had to face in custody determinations.

The courts, fortified with an accumulation of precedents, new legislation, and guidelines often find that the determination in any particular case is fraught with all kinds of difficulties. These difficulties are intensified when the adversaries are buttressed with their own expert witnesses, including mental health professionals, who give conflicting testimony. How does the court weigh one psychiatrist's opinions against another's, for example?

It is in such situations that a family system approach may have special value. Such an approach sets forth principles that are not linked to the claims and counterclaims of contending parents or to the expressed wishes or whims of the children. The family principles center instead on the needs of the whole family as a dynamic system that will continue to have some degree of cohesion beyond the moment of separation or divorce. Such a system examines custody alternatives in terms of criteria that have to do with access among all family members and the continuity of parental responsibility that transcends the divorce decree.

This approach, with its focus on inter-generational relationships, has special significance for the resolution of disputes over child custody. For example, a family psychiatrist ordinarily will study the entire family before making a recommendation to a court on custody and visitation. By studying the entire family and its inter-relationships, rather than with merely one of its members, the family therapist is in a preferred position to make sound evaluations and recommendations. Moreover, such an approach is consistent with the law's concern over so-called "relational interests" which provide the basis for judicial analysis of conflicting and competing interests. In short, an approach that focuses on the whole family is one that appears most compatible with the legal principles involved in child custody cases.

REFERENCES

1. R. S. Weiss, The Emotional Impacts of Marital Separation, *Journal of Social Issues* 32,1 (1976) 135-145.

2. H. H. Foster and D. J. Freed, Joint Custody: Legislative Reform, *Trial* 16,6 (1980) 22-27.

3. R. A. Gardner, PSYCHOTHERAPY WITH CHILDREN OF DIVORCE (New York: Jason Aronson, Inc., 1976) p 381.

4. Bernard Botein, TRIAL JUDGE (New York: Simon and Schuster, 1952) p 273.

5. Robert Gordis, LOVE AND SEX (New York: Farrar, Straus & Giroux, 1978) pp 59-77.

6. Christopher Lasch, THE CULTURE OF NARCISSISM (New York: W. W. Norton, 1978) p 188.

7. Lee Salk, WHAT EVERY CHILD WOULD LIKE PARENTS TO KNOW ABOUT DIVORCE (New York: Harper and Row, 1978) p 95.

8. See note 2, p 23.

2

THE HISTORICAL AND LEGAL BACKGROUND FOR CUSTODY DECISIONS

The prevailing law on child custody mirrors contemporary values shared by the public, although there is usually a lag before the law catches up with social change. For example, the court's decision on what constitutes a "fit" or an "unfit" parent depends largely upon whether or not there is consensus on parental obligations and norms of behavior. In the last century, a parent's sexual "misbehavior" often led courts to conclude that such a parent was unfit to serve as the legal custodian of a child, and vestiges of this attitude remain today. Moreover, the contents of such a general concept as the child's "best interests" may differ from time to time and place to place.

Also the law tends to be responsive to a medical consensus that has relevance for a particular legal issue. Within recent years there have been several examples of legislation sweeping the country after the medical community took a position and made itself heard.[1-3] In addition to influencing legislation, a medical consensus carries great, if not the determinating, weight for court decisions applying common law principles. Thus, generally held theories of child development serve as the basis for many custody decisions. The parental rights premise of earlier law which regarded a child as property has given way to a new approach that stresses the psychological best interests of the child and minimizes parental prerogatives.[4] In the last ten years, increasing emphasis has been placed on the psychological parent-child relationship as distinguished from a biological relationship.[5]

The function of the judge in child custody disputes is to weigh and interpret the conflicting evidence or opinions presented by the parties and to arrive at a decision that accords with the child's best interests. The court considers such matters as the strength and sincerity of the desire for the child's custody; the ability of the claimant to care for the child, especially in light of past performance; the alternative homes and their suitability; and additional matters such as the geographic location of the legal custodian and the child's availability for visitation. In addition, some other factors (e.g., parental fitness), have been stressed so frequently that it is proper to regard them as guidelines for decisions.

Nineteenth century developments

If one were to arbitrarily set the date at which the modern law of custody began, it would be 1817. In that year the poet Percy Bysshe Shelley was involved in a controversy over the custody of his children. He was unfortunate enough to appear before a Lord Eldon, who castigated Shelley's atheistic beliefs as vicious and immoral and denied him custody of his children.[6]

Previously, English law had clearly endorsed the father's paramount right to the custody of his children, regardless of their age or sex. In one case, a Lord Ellenborough ordered the return of a nursing infant to the father whose cruelty had driven the mother and baby from his home, saying he "is the person entitled by law to the custody of his child."[7] After the Shelley case, however, the mother's claim to custody evolved to the point where, in England and in America, she had a preference and a prior right to custody was hers if she was deemed a "fit" parent.

This change during the latter part of the nineteenth century reflected the values introduced by the industrial revolution and the social and moral climate of the times. In place of the feudal order, a new moral order imposing reciprocal rights and duties emerged.[8] Child labor laws and compulsory school attendance statutes were enacted, and the legal status of childhood was extended beyond puberty.[9] Since most children were dependent upon their families, the law imposed a legal duty to support children.

Until the last years of the nineteenth century, a parental-rights premise, derived from feudal and religious principles, underlay custodial law, and was adapted to meet the reciprocal rights and duties fashioned by the Victorian period. Then the concept of "the best interests of the child" gained dominance and became the avowed premise of custodial law. Even in this century, however, traces of the parental-rights doctrine remain, particularly where a custody dispute arises between a parent and a "stranger" (a non-parent).[10]

The test of parental fitness

The social concern over personal morality in the nineteenth century was expressed in court decisions on child custody in terms of parental fitness or unfitness. The temptation to use matrimonial and custodial law to punish sinners and reward the virtuous was irresistible in the nineteenth century and occasionally prevails today. The judicial opprobrium visited upon Shelley in 1817 was repeated in 1897 when Mary Besant, an atheist and noted champion of birth control, was denied custody of her children, even though she and her husband had previously agreed on joint custody.[11] Mary Besant was regarded as an "unfit" parent.

As developed historically and as still largely used today, the term "unfit parent" means *morally* unfit; it does not define ability to parent or to rear a child. Until recently, proof to the satisfaction of the court that a particular parent was "unfit" disqualified that parent from custodianship, while proof of "fitness" ordinarily meant that the fit parent prevailed.[12] Only when the contesting parties were both "fit" was there meaningful consideration of the child's best interests.

Most of the cases in the past ten years have deemed the child's best interests to be the ultimate issue. However, the fitness or unfitness of the parties to custodial disputes has generally been considered relevant in determining best interests, and to some extent it has become a matter of how a court chooses to express its conclusion. For example, some decisions, though phrased in the language of the best interests of the child, have clearly been made on the basis of moral judgments about the competing parents. At other times, it has been clearly stated that placement with an unfit parent would be contrary to the child's best interests. Moreover, parental unfitness, as a legal concept, includes more than sexual misconduct; it is broad enough to encompass abandonment, drunkenness or addiction, and unpopular religious, political, or social beliefs.

Recent decisions, however, have minimized the punitive element implicit in the unfitness concept and have required that alleged unfitness be directly or meaningfully related to child rearing,[13] though vestiges of a moralistic approach still occasionally appear.[14] This is so especially where a liberated lifestyle is flaunted in public. But a change in social values and increased tolerance have led courts to place greater emphasis on the child's welfare and to reevaluate what constitutes parental unfitness.

Gross immorality. Gross immorality that presents an unwholesome influence for children may be both an example of unfitness and an impairment of the child's best interests. Sophisticated courts stress the latter. A New York decision in 1974 held that a divorced mother was entitled to retain custody of her two children (aged six and nine) even though she was a "swinger."[15] There was no proof that the children were affected by her lifestyle; they were found to be happy, well-adjusted, and doing well in school. Moreover, the alternative environment offered by the father was not exemplary.

The same New York court, in 1949, denied custody to a mother who was characterized by the court as a "sexual experimenter" after she defied the court and in effect testified that she would sleep with anybody she cared to.[16] The combination of what was then viewed as an unorthodox lifestyle and her brazenness in court led to a conclusion of her custodial unfitness. At the same time, decisions elsewhere in New York and in other states insisted upon proof that sexual immorality directly affected the child-rearing function.[17] By the 1960's, only Maryland[18] and Nebraska[19] admittedly punished an adulterous mother by withholding child custody, and even those states eventually came to require proof of detriment to the child before a mother's adultery was a basis of disqualifying her from child custody.[20]

Illicit heterosexual activities alone no longer automatically disqualify a party from custodianship. The current conflict in court decisions relates to homosexual relationships and their relevance to custody awards. As early as 1967, a California appellate decision held that homosexuality was not a basis for automatic deprivation of child custody and that the trial court should determine custody in accord with the child's best interests.[21] In 1975, a Washington court permitted two lesbian mothers to retain custody of their children and to maintain a common residence.[22] In 1976, however, a Texas court refused to award child custody to a lesbian mother.[23] These cases illustrate the differences between states and communities in their regard for the relevance of homosexuality to custodial unfitness.

Gross immorality, usually viewed as socially disapproved sexual activity, is still a factor some courts consider in determining custody. Past derelictions are apt to be forgiven if the person, who is alleged to have been guilty of deviant behavior, is repentent before the court.[24] Moreover, with greater social acceptance of various sexual preferences, this consideration increasingly seems to be outweighed by other considerations.

Race and Religion. Although the idea that the custodial parent should "match" the child as nearly as possible in race, color, and religion has been an important concept in child placement cases, it does not often appear in divorce litigation, where the contest is between parents. When it appears, the issue usually relates to the question of adherence to previous agreements (about religion) rather than the issue of matching, per se. Even though the notion of matching has been generally disavowed in placement cases, the criteria for decision making in divorce cases remain unclear. The private convictions of the judge, as well as his prejudices, may serve as unarticulated premises for determining which alternative is best for the child.

In one case, the court reversed custody from the mother to the father when it was shown that she had broken a previous agreement to raise the children in the Jewish faith. After the New Jersey divorce, the non-Jewish mother moved to Idaho and remarried. The nearest temple or Hebrew school was 300 miles from the new home. When the children visited their father in New Jersey, he succeeded in having custody transferred to him because the children were not being reared in the Jewish faith as agreed. In another case, three sons, aged one to four, were awarded to their mother despite her refusal to honor her agreement to raise them in the Catholic faith.[25]

Mental Illness. The current emphasis upon the psychological best interests of the child has led to greater court reliance upon the testimony of mental health experts. The mental health and emotional stability of those seeking custody and the psychological relationship of each to the child is the crucial issue in many child custody cases.[26] Of course, where contending parties produce experts who disagree, the testimony of one may simply cancel out the testimony of the other, and the court may then take what it regards as a common sense approach to the problem.[27] This often means that other considerations will control the court's decision, even though mental health is the crucial question.

The early cases on mental health and child custody were linked to severance of parental rights because of neglect, abuse, etc. Even so, mental illness or emotional instability alone does not establish parental unfitness for child custody.[28] Courts have generally insisted that there be proof the child has been neglected (in the legal meaning of that term) or a showing that there is serious danger of physical injury to the child before a mental patient is disqualified from custody.[29] Moreover, when custodial fitness is the issue, it is the mental or emotional condition *at the time of trial* that is most relevant. If the patient is in a state of remission, he or she may regain custody even though a relapse may be likely.[30] In one case, a schizophrenic mother was awarded custody of her five-year-old son on condition that she submit to psychiatric examinations semi-annually[31]; the assumption was that a check-up twice a year would be sufficient.

One of the earliest decisions stressing the psychological best interests of the child was handed down by a New York court in 1962.[32] The court refused to return a sixteen-year-old son to his mother upon her release from a mental hospital, despite the finding that she had regained competence. During the four years the mother had been hospitalized, the son, while in foster care, had shown marked improvement in school and in his social adjustment. He was no longer "cowed" by a mother described as "aggressive and impatient with her son, and . . . quite unable to control a smothering maternal solicitude which manifests itself in fault-finding and an unwavering determination to impose her views upon him, whether he can profit by her plans or not."[33]

Although the court left the door open for the mother to reapply later for custody, the case is important because at the time of decision there was no clear statutory basis for withholding custody from the mother[34] and because the court held that, upon her recovery, she was not an unfit parent in the usual sense. The mental health of the son and his psychological best interests were the basis for the decision. If the parental-rights doctrine had applied, the court would have reached the opposite result.

In divorce cases, courts are beginning to decide the issue on the basis of the impact of the mental or emotional symptoms on the child in question. As in the neglect cases described above, the mere presence of mental difficulty usually does not result in a disqualification for custody.

Abandonment or relinquishment. While this concept applies primarily to foster care situations, it may also be relevant to divorcing parents. If it is established that a parent has abandoned or relinquished his or her parental rights to a child, various legal consequences may ensue. Abandonment as a concept may be broad enough to cover a failure to maintain suitable contact with a child who is being well cared for by a natural or surrogate parent. A party who has abandoned or deserted a child may thus forfeit claims to custody or visitation. However, "abandonment," although a technical term, is not a precise legal concept, and, if a parent presents justification or a reasonable explanation for lack of contact with the child, the court may accept it.[35] The most frequent example of an apparent abandonment is the one of a mother, who, for economic reasons, places a child with a third person and then later seeks its return.[36]

In a few recent cases, courts have looked at the terms of the placement and its possible temporary character, the efforts made to maintain contact with the child, and the relationship that has developed between the surrogate parents and the child.[37] If the placement was only temporary or justified under the circumstances, it is not regarded as abandonment by most courts.[38]

Modern criteria in child custody cases

In spite of the fact that fathers are beginning to win custody of their children, the mother remains the favorite in custody contests, even when state statutes specify that both parents have equal rights to child custody.[39] One older study estimates that the mother wins at least 90 percent of custody contests with the father,[40] but some observers believe that that proportion is dropping.[41]

The feminist movement and the accompanying drive towards sexual equality have had some impact on child custody litigation. In a few highly publicized cases custody has been awarded to the father over the mother even though she was not an unfit person.[42] But, everything else being equal, or nearly equal, the mother who seeks custody usually gets it because of the common assumption that she is the one best suited to child-rearing. However, there are an increasing number of cases in which permanent custody has been awarded to the father following a period of temporary custody during which things went well.[43] Psychiatric testimony on the quality of the relationship with each parent is especially important if the traditional preference for the mother is to be overcome in a particular case.[44]

The "tender years" doctrine. Associated with the preference for the mother as custodian of the children is the "tender years" doctrine. Formerly, this doctrine resulted in the placement of children under twelve or fourteen with their mother if the family broke up. Recently, some courts have been lowering the age of the child during which the tender years doctrine applies.[45] A few courts have rejected the doctrine altogether on the grounds that it discriminates between parents on the basis of sex.[46] Other courts continue to assume that a young child's welfare is best served by granting custody to the mother if she is a fit person.[47] Such courts retain the traditional preference unless there is clear and convincing evidence to rebut it.

Sex of the child. The preference for the mother also applies in cases where the child whose custody is in dispute is a son rather than a daughter. Courts generally assume that a daughter belongs with her mother but not infrequently rule that a teen-aged son might be better off with his father.[48] Or, in the case of an older boy, parents may be treated equally and the decision made on the facts of the individual case without the aid of any presumption or preference.[49]

Siblings. Courts usually prefer, where possible, to keep siblings together rather than to divide the children between parents.[50] Except in unusual circumstances, courts assume that brothers and sisters ought to be raised together.

Location of custodial parent. Another factor, which sometimes is important, is the preference that the custodial parent continue to live in the state so that the child may have an ongoing relationship with both parents even though they are separated.[51] Courts may express this preference on the basis that it is to the child's best interests for both parents to remain in a particular state or in the United States, and that the particular court retain a continuing jurisdiction over custodial and visitation problems.

Preference of the child. The usual rule is that a child's preference will be considered but that his choice must be a reasonable one before it will be accepted by the court.[52] To have his voice heard, the child must be deemed capable of rational judgment, and the younger he is, the less weight his choice may have in the court's decision.[53] Also, courts are wary of parental efforts to curry favor with the child, particularly in bitterly contested cases.[54] Nevertheless, courts are quite concerned about children's preferences, and judges often chat with children in their chambers, seeking to determine in an indirect fashion their preferences for custody and visitation. This process obviously involves the danger of forcing a child to choose between parents and also the risk that the "in-camera" interview will not accurately reflect the true picture of the child's relationships.[55] Obviously, the interviewing skill of the individual judge is vitally important.

A few states have statutes that require courts to consider the child's preference for custody. A Utah statute, for example, permits a child over ten to choose between rivals for his or her custody.[56] However, the Utah courts have limited that privilege; the child must select a "moral and fit person."[57] Thus, though the child's preference may carry greater weight in Utah than in states that have no such statute, it still must be reasonable in the eyes of the court.

In the case of older children, it may be difficult or impossible to enforce custodial and visitation orders that do not fit their wishes. For example, where custody has been awarded to the mother and visitation to the father, who is also compelled to pay child support, the child may refuse to visit the father, and the father may retaliate by stopping support payments.[58] Unless the visitation and child support provision of the court order or separation agreement are interdependent, and usually they are not, the support obligation continues until the child reaches majority.[59] However, if the mother is deemed to be responsible for the child's negative attitude towards visitation,[60] the father may be held justified in stopping payments unless the child is reduced to seeking public assistance.[61] Counseling is usually more effective than litigation in resolving such situations, but a defiant teen-ager can frustrate the legal rights of the parent who has been awarded custody or visitation. Thus, apart from legal theory, the wishes of an older child ultimately affect the substance of custodial and visitation orders.

Natural parents vs. stepparents or grandparents. Occasionally a stepparent wins a custody dispute with a natural parent. In one Colorado case where, after divorce, the mother who was awarded custody remarried and then died some years later, it was held that the child should remain with the stepfather rather than be uprooted "from her home, her relatives, and from the only stable relationships she has ever known."[62] At the time, in 1962, this was an almost unprecedented decision because the court did not automatically apply the usual legal presumption that a fit natural parent prevails over all others seeking custody. Instead, the Colorado court conceded that the natural father had shown beyond doubt that he was a fit and proper person to have custody, but nonetheless held that the best interests of the child required that custody be continued with the stepfather.[63,64]

A Pennsylvania decision involving grandparents deals with similar issues.[65] Following the divorce of their parents, two daughters were raised in the home of their maternal grandparents until the mother died. The father, who had remarried and had children by his second wife, sought to reclaim the children of his first marriage. In addition to considering the wishes of the children and the psychological parent-child relationship between the children and their grandparents, the court pointed out a possible "Cinderella problem" if the children were forced to live in the father's household. The court referred to

> . . . the *child's* right not to be reared by some other "mother" thrust upon him as a stepparent when he,

himself, may prefer to retain the image of his natural mother. The child may not be desirous of accepting as a mother a stranger chosen arbitrarily by her father. In short, does a child have the right to be reared by his own parent, and if this proves impossible, then to be reared by the person he has long known and loved in the substitute role of parent, rather than by a stranger chosen by his divorced or widowed father or mother?[66]

The Pennsylvania court concluded that the children should remain with the maternal grandparents but that visitation rights would be accorded the father. Its emphasis upon familial interrelationships caused the court to reach a different conclusion from that of a more traditional parental-rights approach.

In the absence of statute, grandparents have no custodial or visitation rights with reference to their grandchildren that courts recognize over parental opposition. However, grandparents who have had *de facto* custody and have been raising a grandchild sometimes succeed in retaining custody, as in Painter v. Bannister.[67] Some twenty or more states have enacted statutes authorizing courts to award visitation rights to grandparents over parental opposition. Some of these statutes are limited to the situation where the grandparents are asserting a claim to custody because of the death or divorce of their offspring who was a parent of the grandchild in question. But scant judicial attention has been given to the psychological needs of a grandchild to maintain a close relationship with grandparents.

Divorce case determination. In previous times, some cases were decided on the principle that the party winning the divorce or separation also won custody of the children,[68] but today only traces of that notion remain. In rare cases, proof of the grounds for divorce may establish parental unfitness for child custody.[69] The more realistic view is that child custody and visitation should be determined independently without regard for marital fault. Of course, the question of who won the divorce is irrelevant for those decrees based on the ground of no-fault or "breakdown of the marriage."

Joint custody. Occasionally, divorce courts award joint custody of children to both parents, although one parent's abode may be considered the preeminent home.[70] In a joint award, each party is a legal custodian, and legal responsibility and parental control are divided. Such an award may prevent either party from winning or losing the custody issue, but the resulting divided authority may produce its own difficulties if the parties cannot succeed in excluding the children from their battles. Some courts, after trying joint custody on an experimental basis, have found that it did not work and have reverted back to custody in one parent.[71] In spite of the various objections to joint custody, there are indications that courts are becoming more willing to consider it experimentally as a demonstration of the equal custodial rights of mothers and fathers,[72] especially when both parents request it.

The publication in 1978 of THE DISPOSABLE PARENT[73] and the 1979 release of KRAMER V. KRAMER,[74] which became a box office hit, precipitated widespread discussion of child custody issues and proposals for legislative change. One such proposal is that there be a statutory presumption in favor of joint custody as the favored alternative. Some states have enacted statutes expressing a preference for joint custody, while other states have rejected such legislation.[75] The presumption is rebuttable and the stated preference is only advisory.

For many years lawyers and mental health professionals rejected joint custody out of hand and assumed it could never work. That assumption is no longer valid. At least where attitudes, logistics, and work schedules are favorable, joint custody is a feasible alternative, and it may be the best substitute that can be offered to replace the intact home. But it should be

remembered that joint custody entails more than shared possession of the child; it also requires shared decision-making and
much effort in the care and upbringing of the child.

Child's best interests vs. parental rights

Perhaps the most important custody case since the English
decision involving Shelley is the 1966 Iowa decision of Painter
v. Bannister.[76] While this case did not arise out of a divorce, it is
relevant to our concerns. Here, parts of an extended family,
once united by marriage, fought over custody of a child after the
original unifying marriage had ended. The father lost custody
of his child to the maternal grandparents. The Supreme Court
refused to review the Iowa decision and let the state court's
judgment stand.[77] The father continued in his efforts to gain
custody and started a suit in California, but the grandparents
eventually capitulated and returned the boy to the father, who
wrote a book about the experience.[78]

Hal Painter, the father of then seven-year-old Mark, was not
found to be an unfit parent, although he suffered in the Iowa
court's comparison with the maternal grandparents. They were
found to be stable citizens of eminent respectability. The Iowa
Supreme Court noted, but did not emphasize, that the placement of Mark with the maternal grandparents had been a
temporary arrangement after Mark's mother and baby sister
had been killed in an automobile accident in Washington in
1962, and Hal Painter had moved to California seeking a job
and a new location. When he had remarried in November 1964,
he asked for Mark's return, but the grandparents refused to give
him up. The father then sought by writ of habeas corpus to
compel Mark's return. Hal Painter had not abandoned or relinquished his claim to Mark and as soon as he could provide a
home, he tried to regain custody. The grandparents had under-

stood the temporary character of the arrangement, and there was no proof that Hal Painter was an unfit parent.

The trial court ruled for the father, but the case was reversed on appeal. Although the Iowa Supreme Court conceded that it was not within its prerogative to determine custody on its choice "of one of two ways of life within normal and proper limits," it insisted that "philosophies are important as they relate to Mark and his particular needs." On that basis, the contrasting lifestyles were held to be relevant, and life with the grandparents was thought to be advantageous for Mark. Hal Painter was described as "either an agnostic or atheist," as a reader of Zen Buddhism, a political liberal, and a member of the American Civil Liberties Union. The home he would provide for Mark, the court believed, would be "unstable, unconventional, arty, Bohemian, and probably intellectually stimulating."[79]

The appellate court placed great reliance upon the testimony of a child psychologist who had examined Mark and the grandparents but not the father.[80] The trial court, incidentally, had rejected the expert opinions and conclusions of this psychologist witness. His testimony was that the grandfather had become the father figure and that Mark had a "very warm feeling for Mr. Bannister."[81] The child psychologist concluded that it was not in Mark's best interests to be removed from the Bannister home and that "the chances are very high [Mark] will go wrong if he is returned to his father."[82] The appellate court gave little if any weight to the parental-rights theory that had dominated much of the common law of custody. Hal Painter's parental rights were cut off in order to secure what the court regarded as the best material and psychological interests of Mark, without regard for the interests of his father, an extreme position for the court to take in the face of well-established precedents.

The American law of custody supports the general proposition that, before a fit parent may be deprived of a child, he or she must have by conduct or agreement relinquished his/her custodial prerogatives.[83] However, if for some reason a parent is deemed unfit, then the best interests of the child may require his placement elsewhere. These principles do not apply where a fit parent has permitted a psychological parent-child relationship to develop between his or her child and others, and has been replaced by the surrogate owing to circumstances beyond his/her control.

A more typical case with a result opposite from Painter v. Bannister is the 1963 Nebraska decision in Raymond v. Cotner.[84] In that case, the parents were divorced when their daughter was an infant, and the mother moved in with her parents, who took care of the child while she worked. The grandparents became the child's psychological parents due to their day-to-day association with the child over the years. When the girl was eleven, the mother was killed. The father, who had remarried and had children by his second wife, sought to regain custody of his daughter. The court admitted that there had been few if any contacts between father and daughter for eleven years and that the grandparents were surrogate parents. The daughter expressed her strong desire to remain with her grandparents and her friends and schoolmates. The court, on the basis of the parental-rights doctrine, held that the father, if a fit parent, had the *exclusive* right to custody.[85] The psychological parent-child relationship which had grown up between the child and her grandparents was disregarded.

Raymond v. Cotner demonstrates the rigidity of an untempered parental-rights approach; Painter v. Bannister, the extreme application of the best-interests theory; the Colorado and Pennsylvania cases cited earlier represent a more reasonable approach.

Legal presumptions

All the criteria discussed above are sometimes put in the form of legal presumptions. For example, a court or a legislature may say that it is to be presumed that the best interests of a child will be served by placement with a natural parent, or that it is presumed that a child of tender years will be better off with its mother. Such presumptions are not conclusive. They are subject to rebuttal. But they do constitute a form of judicial notice of what the law deems to be a general psychological truth. The most effective way of overcoming such presumptions is a strong showing, usually by expert testimony, that the presumption should not hold under the facts of a particular case. For example, proof that a natural parent is unfit, or that the natural mother has abandoned her child, may neutralize the presumptions in favor of the natural parent so that the child's best interests then control the outcome.

Recent statutes affecting custody determinations

The most recent major effort to codify the law of custody is contained in section 402 of the Uniform Marriage and Divorce Act (1971),[86]* which has been adopted in five or more states and has influenced legislation in at least ten other states. The criteria set forth in the act to be considered for awarding child custody include:

- the wishes of the parents
- the wishes of the child
- the interaction and interrelationship of the child with his parent or parents, his siblings, and any other persons
- the child's adjustment to his home, school, and community
- the mental and physical health of all individuals involved.

---

* See Appendix, page 943.

The Uniform Marriage and Divorce Act also provides that the court "shall not consider conduct of a proposed custodian that does not affect his relationship to the child." Subsequent sections authorize interviews, investigations, and reports; there is also cross reference to the Uniform Child Custody Jurisdiction Act* which attempts to preclude "forum shopping" by litigants who take the child from one state to another in the hope of achieving a better outcome. Both Uniform Acts are concerned about maintaining the stability and continuity of the parent-child relationship and cite the literature pertaining to this consideration.

Although several states have recently redrafted statutes regarding child custody, the most detailed statute is Michigan's.[87] It provides that the "best interests of the child" be defined as the sum total of the following factors to be determined by the court.**

- the love, affection, and other emotional ties existing between the competing parties and the child
- the capacity and disposition of competing parties to give the child love, affection, guidance, and continuation of the educating and raising of the child in its religion or creed, if any
- the capacity and disposition of competing parties to provide the child with food, clothing, medical care, or other remedial care
- the length of time the child has lived in a satisfactory, stable environment, and the desirability of maintaining continuity
- the permanence, as a family unit, of the existing or proposed custodial home
- the moral fitness of the competing parties
- the mental and physical health of the competing parties

---

* See Appendix, page 947.
** See Appendix, page 967.

- the home, school, and community record of the child

- the reasonable preference of the child, if the court deems the child to be of sufficient age to express preference

- any other factor considered by the court to be relevant to a particular child custody dispute.

The above criteria probably are the most detailed to be found in any American custody statute and reflect an approach to "best interests" in terms of psychological welfare of the child that is supported by the literature. Furthermore, they are not expressed in terms of absolutes but as criteria to be considered and evaluated. The conscientious application of such criteria should preclude an automatic preference for one parent over the other or a parent over a non-parent; instead, it focuses attention on the necessity to weigh many factors.

A provocative proposal

In 1973, Goldstein, Freud, and Solnit, recommended an approach to the problem of child custody based partly on legal assumptions but largely on psychoanalytic theory and the clinical experience of the authors, two of them child psychoanalysts. Their book, entitled BEYOND THE BEST INTERESTS OF THE CHILD, has resulted in considerable discussion in legal and psychiatric circles because of the authors' prestige and the straightforward simplicity of their recommendations.[88]

They attempted to develop a general concept applicable to all child placement situations, including the child custody issue in divorce, but their case examples primarily involve adoption and foster care. Some observations, however, do seem relevant to all child placement problems. For example, they note especially that the perception of the passage of time in a child's life is different from that for an adult—that the younger the child, the more the child's "sense of time" makes it difficult to delay the solution to distressing problems. The young child, in a sense, cannot wait. They conclude that speed in the settlement after divorce is essential.

They also develop the concept of the "psychological parent"—the person, who by his or her caring for the child's needs, develops a reciprocal psychological relationship with the child. Although their work has been recommended for strongly supporting that concept and focusing attention upon the psychological needs of children, that concept is applicable mainly in foster care and adoption, as is the issue of the "wanted child."

Based on their "value preference" for privacy, they feel that custody determinations should be final.

> To safeguard the right of parents to raise their children as they see fit, free of government intrusion, except in cases of neglect and abandonment, is to safeguard each child's need for continuity. This preference for minimum state intervention and for leaving well enough alone is reinforced by our recognition that law is incapable of effectively managing, except in a very gross sense, so delicate and complex a relationship as that between parent and child.[89]

In the settlement of child custody problems in divorce when the parents cannot agree, Goldstein, Freud, and Solnit would award custody to one parent and allow that parent to control the contact with the other.

> Children have difficulty in relating positively to, profiting from, and maintaining the contact with two psychological parents who are not in positive contact with each other. Loyalty conflicts are common and normal under such conditions and may have devastating consequences by destroying the child's positive relationships to both parents. A "visiting" or "visited"

parent has little chance to serve as a true object for love,
trust, and identification, since this role is based on his
being available on an uninterrupted day-to-day basis.

Once it is determined who will be the custodial parent, it is that parent, not the court, who must decide
under what conditions he or she wishes to raise the
child. Thus, the noncustodial parent should have no
legally enforceable right to visit the child, and the custodial parent should have the right to decide whether it
is desirable for the child to have such visits. What we
have said is designed to protect the security of an ongoing relationship—that between the child and the custodial parent. At the same time the state neither makes nor
breaks the psychological relationship between the child
and the noncustodial parent, which the adults involved
may have jeopardized. It leaves to them what only they
can ultimately resolve.[90]

These suggestions have been subject to legal criticism on
several grounds. The main concern is about the absolute and
extreme positions advocated.[91] According to Foster, "It is indeed unfortunate that a matrimonial lawyer was brought in to
temper and qualify some of the assumptions and statements in
this book."[92] He goes on to summarize the legal objections, as
follows:

Courts cannot and will not abdicate from the *parens
patriae* or wardship responsibilities they have assumed.
They will not abandon continuing jurisdiction over
custodial and placement matters, as advocated by the
authors, because there should be a running check even
though we favor an emphasis upon the factor of continuity. A veto power over visitation rights will be rejected because from the legal viewpoint the dissolution
of a marriage does not terminate the parent-child relationship, and the child ordinarily needs and is entitled
to an ongoing relationship with both parents. Most
courts will continue to require parental relinquish-

ment of the child before they consider either the best interests or least detrimental alternative tests. Even though a state adopts no-fault divorce, they will shy away from no-fault termination of parental rights.[93]

In addition to the legal concerns about this work, there are also serious questions about some of the psychiatric assumptions on which it is based. These will be taken up in the next chapter.

Most courts strive to reach a fair and sound result in custody disputes and conscientiously weigh and balance the evidence, which is often conflicting. It is a great comfort to the judge to be aware that his decision is always subject to modification upon substantial change in custodial circumstances. Such is the law in every state.[94] Custody decrees, therefore, are pragmatic, and if a particular order turns out to be ill-advised, it is subject to change in order to come closer to the best interests of the child. Although this possibility of modification entails some threat to the security and stability of custodial arrangements, it may be justified bcause it permits error to be corrected. Equally important, it allows the court in the first instance to act more expeditiously on an urgent matter because of the knowledge that its decision may be modified if necessary.

It should be noted that policies and principles pertaining to child custody operate within a particular setting. Although sometimes a custody award may be made in a habeas corpus action, bill in equity, or some other kind of proceeding, most often an initial custody award is made in conjunction with a divorce or dissolution case. Over 90 percent of divorce cases are uncontested. Where middle or upper-income clients are involved, these uncontested cases are usually preceded by separation agreements, settlements, or contracts negotiated by lawyers. The divorce hearing itself is a *pro forma* matter. Usually the court's decree incorporates the terms the parties have agreed

upon. Therefore, it is the negotiation process, including custody and visitation, rather than the court hearing, that is most
crucial for the resolution of disputed issues.

Thus, statutes and prior court decisions regarding custody
have their most frequent and useful application during the
negotiation process. Such law sets the basis for parental give
and take, providing leverage and guidelines to the negotiating
parties. Because of this process, the children of divorce may
need independent representation as many have suggested.
What may really be most useful, since the majority of cases are
uncontested, is a court administrator who checks on the negotiated terms of custody, visitation, and child support from the
point of view of the child's interests. In addition, in the less
frequent case that is contested, the child may need independent
counsel to guarantee that his welfare is not overlooked in the
adversary struggle.[95]

Courts and legislatures, however, are reluctant to mandate
the provision of counsel for children because of the expense, the
counterweight of tradition, and the fear that such counsel
might exacerbate the proceedings.[96] At present, probably the
most that can be hoped for is the granting of discretionary
authority to appoint counsel for children in custody cases, as
specified in the Uniform Marriage and Divorce Act.[97]

Another feature of custody disputes merits notice. There are
vast differences between lawyers who practice matrimonial law
and those who practice custodial law. At one extreme are those
who function primarily as counselors; at the other extreme are
the inveterate litigators. In handling divorce and custody matters, some lawyers explore in detail the alternatives for reaching
agreement, seeking therapy, or trying arbitration. They view
their duty as one to the whole client in terms of long-range
advantage, with due consideration for intra-family relationships. The aggressive lawyer, on the other hand, battles on

behalf of his client to press for immediate advantages. Some clients who are not in a compromising mood seek out this sort of lawyer. Most lawyers, of course, fall somewhere between these extremes.

In those few custody disputes that go to a contested trial, the lawyer's role in court is properly that of a partisan. In essence, the system requires that he examine and cross-examine witnesses forcefully and vigorously. But the adversary process works only if all parts of the system perform their assigned tasks. In Painter v. Bannister,[98] the system did not function optimally because opposing counsel did not properly cross-examine the psychologist expert witness and instead permitted him to testify extensively without challenging the basis for his testimony. The trial transcript, which was the basis for the successful appeal, did not show a clear picture of the limitations of his testimony or of the admittedly speculative nature of much of his evidence.

The problems that vex the trial judge must also be considered. In many cases, there are too few hard data to provide a basis for informed decision. The judge is ordinarily limited to the record before him, and it is difficult for him to compensate for the inadequacies of trial counsel or witnesses. Courts differ in their willingness to order staff investigations and reports to supplement the record, and facilities for such services also vary from court to court. Furthermore, if a judge has strong convictions about child-rearing or a bias for or against a particular theory of child development, the facts available may be filtered through those preconceptions. Most judges strive to eliminate personal bias and to protect the best interests of children; nevertheless, in some instances, the judge's tacit convictions help shape the resulting decision.

Although it is probably impossible to define accurately the psychological assumptions that underlie judicial functioning, a few generalizations may be ventured. First of all, the individual judge's personal point of view is enormously important in custody decisions. One legal observer stated it as follows:

> . . . one must always bear in mind that the exercise of discretion by a judge is far less a product of his learning than of his personality and his temperament, his background and his interests, his biases and prejudices, both conscious and unconscious.[99]

Secondly, the judges tend to share a similar cultural value orientation. For example, a substantial portion of the judiciary hearing custodial issues are middle-age, middle class males. Their value systems reflect their age and status, and they may resist change. Eventually, however, social changes that are shared by a substantial group in the population are reflected in court decisions. Legal decisions do bend to cultural changes, including new psychological insights.[100]

One example is the increasing reluctance of courts to change custody unless there are substantial and convincing reasons to modify an earlier custody decree. Courts have heard and have been convinced by arguments regarding the importance of continuity, stability, and security of family relationships for a child's healthy development. Courts are concerned about potential harm to the child and the psychological best interests of children.[101] In contested custody cases, however, courts are also concerned about justice to the contesting parties and do not make judicial determinations solely in terms of clinical evaluations.

Nevertheless, the courts recognize that psychiatric principles and theories are highly relevant. Since the "best interests of the child" standard is very broad and is claimed as the basis for decision, regardless of the result,[102] it is important to be aware of the secondary criteria that often enter into the court's determination of best interests. Traditional criteria have included those bearing on fitness for custody. The trend now, however, is that misconduct must have some direct relation to child rearing to be relevant. The emotional stability and mental health of the contestants and the child are significant considerations and take precedent over such subordinate concerns as relative resources, living conditions, and the lifestyles of the contestants.

What is it that judges want from the expert mental health professional? The responsibility of choosing between competing parties is aided by informed judgments. In many cases the court will need relevant psychiatric information about the behavior and personalities of all concerned, their interaction with each other, and the psychological effect each alternative will probably have upon the child. In some instances, the court will want to know whether or not joint custody may be a workable solution. Most of all, the court wants information as it relates to the specific parties involved rather than general theory.

Unlike court decisions in many if not most countries, the courts in the United States traditionally set forth the grounds for decision in opinions by the court. This serves two purposes: it facilitates a thoughtful conclusion, and it makes a record for an appeal. If the grounds given for the result cannot withstand scrutiny, the trial judge may be reversed, which may be a blow to his pride and dignity.

Finally, it should be noted that legal process deals with the resolution of individual disputes within a structure of judicially determined relevance. A particular decision may, however, have far-reaching consequences and may establish social policy for situations far removed from the original case.

REFERENCES

1. A. Sussman and S. Cohen, REPORTING CHILD ABUSE AND NEGLECT (Cambridge: Ballinger, 1975) p 59.

2. Beginning in 1959 in California, so-called "Good Samaritan" statutes were enacted in over 40 states. Although these statutes differ, the general purpose is to grant to physicians, who undertake to render emergency first aid, immunity from civil suits unless gross negligence is present.

3. The Uniform Anatomical Gift Act was approved by the Commissioners on Uniform State Laws in 1968 and was passed by almost all of the states since then. For the beneficial effect of the act in encouraging kidney donations, see *Eleventh Report of the Renal Transplant Registry* 226:1197 (1973).

4. A. Bradbook, The Relevance of Psychological and Psychiatric Studies to the Future Development of the Law Governing the Settlement of Inter-Paternal Child Custody Disputes, *Journal of Family Law* 11:557 (1972). See also John Batt, Child Custody Disputes: A Developmental-Psychological Approach to Proof and Decision Making, *Willamette Law Journal* 12:491 (1976).

5. J. Goldstein, Anna Freud, and A. J. Solnit, BEYOND THE BEST INTERESTS OF THE CHILD (New York: The Free Press, 1973).

6. Shelley v. Westbrooke, 37 Eng. Rep. 850 (Ch. 1817).

7. King v. DeManneville, 102 Eng. Rep. 1054 (K. B. 1804).

8. See Roscoe Pound, THE FORMATIVE ERA OF AMERICAN LAW (Boston: Little, Brown, 1938); and Karl Llewellyn, THE COMMON LAW TRADITION (Boston: Little, Brown, 1960).

9. See J. Holt, ESCAPE FROM CHILDHOOD (New York: Ballantine, 1974).

10. But see Justice Joseph Story's decision in United States v. Green, 3 Mason 482, Fed Cas. No. 15, 256 (Cir R.I. 1824); Brinster v. Compton, 68 Ala. 229 (1824); and Chapsky v. Wood, 26 Kan. 650, 40 Am. Rep. 321 (1881), all of which were remarkable because of

the court's greater concern with the child's welfare than with blood relationships.

11. In re Besant (1879) 11 Ch. D. 508, C.A.

12. See H. Simpson, The Unfit Parent, *University of Detroit Law Journal* 39:347 (1962).

13. For example, see Feldman v. Feldman, 45 A.D.2d 320, 358 N.Y.S.2d 507 (2d Dept. 1974).

14. For example, In re R.D.H.S., 370 S.W.2d 661 (Mo. App. 1963), denied custody to a mother who objected to testimony that she was "slightly" promiscuous, saying that she had had many acts of intercourse with her lover and other men.

15. See Feldman v. Feldman, supra, note 13.

16. Bunim v. Bunim, 298 N.Y. 391, 83 N.E.2d 848 (1949).

17. "Adultery assumes the stature of a bar [to child custody] only if coupled with other traits like running off with the husband's drunken brother. . . . If the adulterous wife regularly entertains paramours in her home, she is usually out of luck. . . . Even so, she may still win part-time custody, despite her bad habits, as in one case where the mother admitted illicit relations every Saturday night. The children were supposed to be upstairs asleep, though on one occasion one of them came down and found 'mom wiggling on the couch with a man.' " B. Small, "Family Law," *1964 Annual Survey of American Law* (1965) 491-492.

18. Maryland formerly denied custody to an adulterous mother in most cases, but in Ouellette v. Ouellette, 246 Md. 604, 229 A.2d 129, 23 A.L.R.3d 1 (1967), it was held that the fact that the mother had committed adultery was not an absolute bar and that the best interests of the children were the primary concern.

19. The Nebraska rule formerly was that adultery was an absolute bar to custody, but that rule was relaxed in Morrissey v. Morrissey, 154 N.W.2d 66 (Neb. 1967).

20. The "Comment," Effect of Adultery on Custody Awards, *Washington and Lee Law Review* 16:287 (1959), says that, prior to the 1920's, Massachusetts appears to be the only state that has awarded custody of a child to an adulterous mother while the

more recent cases reflect a majority view that such a mother may prevail if she is regarded as reformed or a fit person at the time of the trial.

21. Nadler v. Superior Court, 63 Cal. Rptr. 352 (Cal. App. 1967). See also, Commonwealth ex rel. Bachman v. Bradley, 171 Pa. Super. 587, 91 A.2d 379 (1952).

22. The case is cited in *Playboy*, 22,5 (1975) 59.

23. The case is cited in *Playboy*, 23,5 (1976) 46.

24. Brown v. Ellinson 162 So.2d 805 (La. App. 1964), State v. Marusak, 205 So.2d 477 (La.App. 1967); and "Comment," Effect of Adultery in Custody Awards, *Washington and Lee Law Review* 16:287 (1959).

25. T. v. H., 102 N.J. Super. 38, 245A.2d 221 (1968); Begley v. Begley, 13 A.D.2d 961, 216 N.Y.S.2d 417 (1961), aff'd 12 N.Y.2d 691, 185 N.E.2d 912 (1962).

26. J. DuCanto, Mental Illness and Child Custody, *Journal of Family Law* 7:637 (1967).

27. For example, see Portewig v. Ryder, 160 S.E.2d 89 (Va. 1968).

28. See Application of Richman, 30 Misc.2d 1090, 227 N.Y.S. 42 (1962); and Todd v. Superior Court, 414 P.2d 605 (Wash. 1966).

29. See J. DuCanto, Mental Illness and Child Custody, *Journal of Family Law* 7:636 (1967).

30. Ibid.

31. Application of Richman, supra, note 28.

32. Application of Mittenthal, 37 Misc. 2d 502, 235, N.Y.S.2d 729 (Fam. Ct. 1962).

33. 235 N.Y.S.2d at 736.

34. At the time of the Mittenthal decision (1962), the applicable provision of the N.Y. Fam. Ct. Act was 312 which defined a "neglected" child but made no reference to impairment of a child's mental health.

35. See A. Oster, Custody Proceeding: A Study in Vague and Indefinite Standards, *Journal of Family Law* 5:21 (1965).

36. Ibid. Compare, Matter of Vanderbilt, 245 App. Div. 211, 281 N.Y.S. 171 (1935), where the mother sought to reclaim Gloria Vanderbilt, then ten years old, from the aunt who had been caring for her. The court found that long continued indifference of the mother constituted abandonment but that the mother was entitled to visitation rights. Another similar tragedy is that recounted by Brenda Frazier in her article, My Debut—A Horror, *Life* 55:136 (Dec. 1963). See also, Rockefeller v. Murphy, 152 N.Y.L.J. 19, Oct. 2, 1964, for the decision in the "Happy" Rockefeller case.

37. See In re Adoption of a Child by P. and Wife, 114 N.J. Super. 584, 277 A.2d 566 (1971); and In re Revocation of Appointment of a Guardian, 271 N.E.2d 621 (Mass. 1971).

38. "The cases indicate that relinquishment or abandonment of the child is the strongest factor which may overcome judicial preference for the mother. Psychologically, this is required as an 'unnatural' act, contrary to the instincts of motherhood, and the strongest evidence of maternal unfitness. When a wife lives apart from her husband and children, without just cause, she may forfeit all claim to custody. In such cases, although there is a tendency to adopt a punitive approach, the question should be whether the act of abandonment necessarily reveals indifference to their welfare . . ." H. Foster and D. Freed, LAW AND THE FAMILY—NEW YORK, I (Rochester, NY: Lawyers Cooperative, 1972) pp 509-510.

39. For example, N.Y. Dom. Rel. L. Section 70 provides that there shall be no *prima facie* right to the custody of children but that the court shall determine what is for the best interests of the child.

40. See R. Drinan, The Rights of Children in Modern American Family Law, *Journal of Family Law* 2:101 (1962).

41. Elissa P. Benedek, Personal Communication, Oct. 30, 1978.

42. Salk v. Salk, 393 N.Y.S. 2d 841, Aff'd 385 N.Y.S. 2d 1015 (1976) found that both parents were fit and loving but that the father, an eminent child psychologist, was better able to give the children "superior cultural and emotional advantages."

43. Joseph Satten, Personal Communication, Nov. 9, 1979.

44. See S. Kram and N. Frank, The Future of Tender Years, *Trial* 12:14 (April 1976).

45. In Kentucky, for example, it is reported that the cut-off age for the "tender years" doctrine is as low as six years. See REPORT OF SEMINAR ON DOMESTIC RELATIONS, February 22-23, 1974, p. 55, prepared by the Office of Continuing Legal Education, University of Kentucky College of Law.

46. See State *ex rel.* Watts v. Watts, 350 N.Y.S.2d 285 (Fam Ct. 1973); D'Addario v. D'Addario, N.Y.L.J., Jan. 8, 1976; Matter of Barry Wynn, N.Y.L.J., Jan 6, 1976; Pratt v. Pratt, 330 N.E.2d 244 (Ill. App. 1975); Marcus v. Marcus, 320 N.E.2d 581 (Ill. App. 1974); Davis v. Davis, 261 P.2d 729 (Cal. 1953); and Holsinger v. Holsinger, 279 P.2d 961 (Cal. 1955).

47. For example, see Commonwealth *ex rel.* Lucas v. Kreischer, 299 A.2d 243 (Pa. 1973), and Commonwealth *ex rel.* Spriggs v. Carson, 323 A.2d 273 (Pa. 1974). Alabama applies the "tender years" doctrine by statute. See Code of Ala. 1940, as Recompiled, 1958, Title 34 and 35.

48. "The sex of the child may be relevant, the courts usually finding that the interests of a girl are best served by being in her mother's custody, while those of a boy old enough to no longer require his mother's constant care are best served by being in his father's custody." H. Clark, LAW OF DOMESTIC RELATIONS (St. Paul: West, 1968) p 585.

49. Ibid.

50. Ibid., pp 586-587.

51. Ibid.

52. Clark says, "If the child is old enough to form an intelligent judgment about his own custody his choice will be given weight. In some states, by statute compliance with the child's wishes is mandatory if he has reached a prescribed age, which is fourteen in most states." Compare, People v. Glendening, 259 App. Div. 384, 19 N.Y.S.2d 693 (Sup. Ct. 1940), where the court disregarded

a sixteen-year-old son's preference to be with his mother, when he had lived with the father for eleven years.

53. Clark says, "Where the age of discretion is not established by statute, the cases do not lay down absolute rules, but give more or less weight to the child's desires depending upon his age. The desires of a six-year-old boy do not weigh heavily with the court, while those of a twelve-year-old boy do."

54. For example, see Allen v. Allen, 200 Ore. 678, 268 P.2d 358 (1954).

55. See Kreutzer v. Kreutzer, 266 Ore. 158, 359 P.2d 536 (1961); Lincoln v. Lincoln, 24 N.Y.2d 270, 299 N.Y.S.2d 842, 247 N.E.2d 659 (1969).

56. Utah Code Ann., 1953, 130-3-5.

57. Smith v. Smith, 15 Utah 2d 36, 386 P.2d 900 (1963).

58. See note 48, p 504.

59. Ibid., p 505. "The clearest ground for modification of child support orders is that the child has reached twenty-one, except in those rare cases where the child remains unable to care for himself due to physical or mental illness . . . Likewise the emancipation of the child is a ground for terminating the order for support." Note, however, that in some states the age of majority now is age eighteen, and depending upon statutory construction, the support duty may then end at eighteen, or, if the statutes are clear, continued until twenty-one.

60. Ibid., p 504. "Though the child cannot be allowed to go without support because of his mother's misconduct, the support payments may be reduced or cut off for her violation where she has sufficient funds to support the child so that the modification will not prejudice the child's welfare." See also N.Y. Dom. Rel. Law section 241 which permits a court to terminate alimony or child support if visitation rights are interfered with.

61. See H. Foster and D. Freed, LAW AND THE FAMILY—NEW YORK, (Rochester, NY: Lawyers Cooperative, 1966) II p 543.

62. Root v. Allen, 151 Colo. 311 P.2d 117 (1962).

63. 377 P.2d at 120.

64. See note 48, p 877.

65. In re Custody of Hampton, 5 Adams Co. L.J. 84 (Pa. C.P. 1963).

66. Ibid.

67. See note 76 below.

68. Wells v. Wells, 117 S.W.2d 700 (Mo. App. 1938); "Comment," Custody and Control of Children, *Fordham Law Review* 5:460 (1936).

69. See cases collected in 23 A.L.R.3d 6.

70. See note 48, pp 590-591.

71. For example, see Gardner v. Pettit, 192 So. 2d 696 (Miss. 1967). See also "Note," Divided Custody of Children After Their Parents Divorce, *Journal of Family Law* 8:58 (1968). Until recently, only one state, North Carolina, had a statute specifically providing for divided custody (N.C. Gen. Stat. 50-13 [1953]), although no state specifically forbade it by statute. Recently, statutes have been enacted in a number of states which authorize joint custody or give it priority as an alternative. Such states include Alaska, Arkansas, California, Iowa, Kansas, Nevada, Oregon, Texas, and Wisconsin. See H. Foster and D. Freed, *Trial* 16:22 (1980).

72. One consideration that may lead to divided custody is "the need of a small son to know and have the companionship of his father." See Mason v. Zolonsky, 103 N.W.2d 752 (Iowa 1960). Another is the parents' agreement on divided custody. See Flanagan v. Flanagan, 247 P.2d 212 (Ore. 1952). So too, the strains of divided custody are minimized where the homes of prospective custodians are similar and in the same neighborhood. See "Note," supra, *Journal of Family Law* 8:58, 65 (1968).

73. M. Roman and W. Haddad, THE DISPOSABLE PARENT (New York: Holt, Rinehart & Winston, 1978).

74. Columbia Pictures, KRAMER VS. KRAMER, 1979, based on a book by Avery Corman. KRAMER VERSUS KRAMER (New York: Random House, 1977).

75. See note 71.

76. 258 Iowa 1390, 140 N.W.2d 152 (1966).

77. Cert. denied 385 U.S. 949 (1966).

78. H. Painter, MARK, I LOVE YOU (New York: Simon & Schuster, 1967).

79. 140 N.W.2d at 155.

80. 140 N.W.2d at 154.

81. 140 N.W.2d at 156.

82. Ibid. Professor Henry Foster served on a panel with Dr. Glen R. Hawks, the child psychologist who was the expert witness in Painter v. Bannister, and discussed with him Dr. Hawk's testimony in the case. According to Dr. Hawks (and the transcript of his testimony confirms it), there was virtually no control over his testimony by either counsel at the trial, and he speculated freely, drawing conclusions that he could not substantiate had he been challenged. The case is discussed at length in H. Foster, Adoption and Child Custody; Best Interests of the Child? *Buffalo Law Review* 22:1 (1972).

83. Ibid.

84. 175 Neb. 158, 120 N.W.2d 892 (1963).

85. See dissenting opinion in Raymond v. Cotner, 120 N.W. at 896. In a subsequent decision, the Nebraska court modified its extreme position. See In re Application of Carlson, 181 Neb. 877, 152 N.W.2d 98, 25 A.L.R.3d 1 (1967).

86. For a discussion of the Uniform Act, see Symposium on Uniform Marriage and Divorce Act, *South Dakota Law Review* 18:531 (1973). See also H. Foster and D. Freed, Divorce Reform: Brakes on Breakdown? *Journal of Family Law* 13:3, 443-489 (1974).

87. Mich. Stat. Ann. 25.312(3) (Supp. 1972).

88. See note 5.

89. Ibid., p 8.

90. Ibid., p 38.

91. One of the first cases to cite and rely upon BEYOND THE BEST INTERESTS OF THE CHILD was State *ex rel.* Watts v. Watts, 350

N.Y.S.2d 285 (Sup. Ct. 1974). However, the court, in Pierce v. Yerkovich, 80 Misc. 2d 613, 363 N.Y.S.2d 403 (Fam. Ct. 1974), rejected as "specious" the argument that the legal custodian should have veto rights over visitation with the other parent, even though Dr. Solnit appeared in the case as a witness and endeavored to support that argument.

92. The book has been widely read and reviewed, but see criticism by H. Foster, *Bulletin of the American Academy of Psychiatry and the Law* 2:46 (1974), reprinted in *Willamette Law Journal* 12:545 (1976); P. Strauss and J. Strauss, *Columbia Law Review* 74:996 (1974); and *Child Welfare* 53:189 (1974).

93. See first reference in note 92, p 48.

94. H. Foster, A BILL OF RIGHTS FOR CHILDREN (Springfield, IL: Charles C Thomas, 1974) pp 42-45, 70-71.

95. Ibid.

96. For example, Connecticut, which had statutory provisions for providing independent counsel for children in custody cases, recently repealed that law upon the conclusion that it was not functional.

97. Section 310 of the Uniform Marriage and Divorce Act.

98. See notes 76 and 82.

99. H.M. Fain, Family Law—Whither Now? *Journal of Divorce* 1:1 (1977) 31.

100. C. Winick, I. Gerver, and A. Blumberg, "The Psychology of Judges," C6 in LEGAL AND CRIMINAL PSYCHOLOGY by Hans Toch (New York: Holt, Rinehart and Winston, 1962), Chapter 10, pp 121-145.

101. The "Comment" in *Yale Law Journal* 73:151 (1963), stressing psychological best interests, has been widely cited and quoted. So too, A. Watson, The Children of Armageddon: Problems of Custody Following Divorce, *Syracuse Law Review* 21:55 (1969).

102. For example, see People *ex rel.* Scarpetta v. Spence-Chapin Adoption Services, 28 N.Y.2d 185, 269 N.E. 787, 321 N.Y.S.2d 65 (1971).

3

THE FAMILY PERSPECTIVE

The family approach to life's problems aims at establishing more satisfying ways of living for the entire family, *not only for a single family member*. Focusing on the whole family, this approach places major emphasis on understanding individual behavior patterns in relation to the complicated matrix of the family as an interacting system. This view is especially useful in situations where the family faces major change. In the following paragraphs we introduce some of the assumptions family clinicians make in their approach to understanding the family's experience of divorce.

The family as a system

A family is bound together by intense and long-lasting ties of past experience, social roles, mutual support, and expectations. It constitutes an interactive milieu in which transactions between individual family members are continually taking place. The action of any one member affects the whole family. A ripple set up anywhere, internally or externally, makes itself felt through the entire system.

The family and individual development

All members of a family in large measure derive their sense of who they are and who they may become from their knowledge and experience of their relationship with other members of the family. Although other groups of which they are members are important—friendships, work groups, and so forth—family ties are especially vital to development. We first learn who we are as we discover ourselves as infants and children in the families into which we are born. We learn who we may become as we develop our sexual and responsible selves in the families into which we marry, have children, and take our greatest care of others.

The sense of ourselves that we work out in these families is built up out of constantly developing relationships: dependencies, obligations, alliances, antagonisms, teachings and learnings, and communications of all kinds. These are understood, or at least sensed, by all members of the family. They can best be described by people in cultures where *kinship* is explicitly a basis of organization. For example, a boy in a South Sea Islands village can tell exactly what his obligations are to his maternal grandfather; he knows he will be taught certain things and punished in certain ways by his mother's brother; he understands that he may not openly insult his older brother. All of these are part of the conscious general rules of his society. He and his American counterpart also know some idiosyncratic rules—rules that apply in one family but not in others: that his mother is being affectionate when she teases him although she does not tease his little sister; that his father expects him not to cry in his presence. There are also some realizations outside his awareness: he may not know that his father sometimes envies him his freedom and license as a little boy, but he registers that fact somewhere. Perhaps he will not become aware of it until he later feels himself unaccountably angry with his own son.

This last example—the learning of fathering or mothering from one's experience of being a child—emphasizes the importance of *developmental stages* in family life for the determination of the relevance of structure and interaction. Much has been written (by Erikson,[1] for example) about the age-appropriate "crises" or passages of adolescence and middle life—adolescents breaking away, older parents turning away from children and towards, or away from, each other. The saying that "there is a time for holding and a time for letting go" refers to the changing patterns of attachment in the family which are age-specific.

Young children appear to be especially sensitive to these patterns of attachment. Newborns (see Bowlby[2] and, Rutter[3]) seem to require some period of bonding with a mother figure or figures in order to develop the most elementary kind of social reciprocity later in life. There is epidemiological evidence (see Dohrenwend and deFiguerido[4] and Brown and Harris[5]) that children who suffer the death of a parent between ages six and eleven are especially vulnerable to depression when faced with losses in later life. The clinical experience of psychoanalysts and other therapists has been that the model for the constancy of relationships that the child receives at early stages of life will be applied to later choices of intimate relationships. The model consists not only of the one or two most important parental relationships considered one at a time, but also of the whole interlocking structure and ambience of the family in its setting. Parents—even, or especially, divorcing parents—have a responsibility for continuing to construct this emotional universe for their young children.

The regulation of stability and change

In both their official and their unacknowledged rules or norms, family relations have a certain balance and constancy. In some cultures, for example, the wife's family gives a dowry in exchange for her support. Until recently in America, women exchanged child care and household work for the husband's support, and children exchanged obedience for nurture.

There is another kind of balance that is less conscious but perhaps for this very reason more powerful—the unspoken rules of group behavior. A husband and wife may frequently fight when they are alone together because that is the only way they can keep from talking seriously. A man may get drunk whenever his wife visits her mother's house; he may deny it, but the children expect it and arrange to be out of the way when it happens. A husband may sense by the atmosphere in the house when his wife is willing to make love with him, but he may not know it consciously. He may also counteract her offer without knowing it: by becoming busy, he conceals from himself that he is refusing to go to bed.

These are examples of homeostasis, or self-regulatory behavior, in a family group. They tend to run in patterns, to return the course of life to familiar limits, as a buffer against change. The conservatism of the family in this respect resembles stable tendencies in other groups.

Opposing this conservatism are the institutions of the family that promote and manage change. The marriage that starts a new family is in itself a major change for the bride and groom, and for the families they leave behind. And so it is with the birth and growth of children, their independence and marriage, the onset of grandparenthood, retirement, and in leaving their spouses and others in illness and in death. These changes all tend to be marked or in some way acknowledged by the family itself. If they are not so marked, family members cannot deal with them emotionally in an effective manner. These changes need to be recognized as occasions for growth, but also of danger, of strain, and of loss or separation from some family member. The family must also reorganize itself around the changes.

Most such changes have a turning point—a moment officially marked as the time when the relations alter or when the loss occurs irreparably, usually acknowledged by a ceremony or rite of passage. At weddings and funerals, for example, members of the extended family gather to affirm their new relationships to the principals and to the others. And, aside from the ceremonies, the family members generally have some preparation for the event. The communicating network of the family is alive with talk and consultations for the upcoming wedding, or birth, or graduation, or there is concern about someone's serious illness. The communication is expected and tends to have a certain openness to all concerned.

Divorce as a special form of change

Divorce belongs to a class of changes in family relations for which there is no good way to prepare, especially for the most immediate participants. Since it is not normally supposed to happen, the family neither prepares for it, nor mourns it officially. For the children, especially, there are no official rites attending divorce which help to give it meaning. In this respect, divorce is like a sudden death. Death, however, has a finality that can often be worked through with the help of others once it has been accepted. On the other hand, divorce still carries the possibility or the fantasy of the broken family being restored, especially for the children. The members are, after all, separated only by anger, and children have always understood that anger does not last forever. In this way, divorce breaks a child's major intrafamilial rule—forgiveness. Without forgiveness, he/she either feels the hurt of being rejected or the guilt of being the rejector.

Divorce is an especially unmanageable catastrophe, also, because talking about it, expecting it, or understanding one's feelings about it, are inhibited by the splits of loyalty it involves. Certain otherwise natural thoughts or communications are thwarted, and to that extent divorce becomes harder to manage. A son who lives with his mother and is forbidden to see his father may be required by her to be loyal to her side of the dispute. He then has to deny his own wish to see and understand his father or risk his relationship with his mother. There are, of course, other crises that are unmanageable because of thwarted communications—for example, a death that cannot be mourned because a person loses a parent he is expected to hate or a young person's electing a homosexual way of life that his parents find too threatening to discuss. Professionals can sometimes help in these crises by exploring the feelings of participants and by helping them communicate with each other and with other family members. Such efforts can also help children and others involved in a divorce.

Open communication as the context of change

For children, the sense of loss cuts especially deep because so much of the task of a child's growing up centers around the ordering of attachments and separation. The psychoanalytic study of children has shown that a whole series of experiences are necessary for the growth and maturation of children through the steps that lead them to an adult life of emotional maturity and responsibility. Ideally, these changes of attachment take place in an atmosphere of support, clarity, and thoughtfulness on the part of others involved. In the classical case of the "resolution of the Oedipus complex," for example, the four-to-five-year-old boy moves from a primary attachment to his mother, in which he imagines that he might possess her exclusively, to a rivalrous comparison of himself and his father. From this point he proceeds to an attachment to his father through realizing the commonality of many of their interests, and to a realistic recognition of his relationship to both parents. This requires that his mother indicate to him that she is not available as the figure in his fantasies, that she show her approval of his developing relationship with his father—and it is important that mother and father demonstrate a separate stability of their relationship that is independent of the child—and that the boy have enough access to his father in daily life to be able to experience him, in some way, as a model and companion.

All of this requires *access*, direct experience, and openness of communication. The same is true of other stages of development: the movement of the child from family to school friends, to more independent adolescent group experiences, to falling in love, and so on. The social forms and family attitudes that surround these enterings and leavings of the child's close attachments are all of prime importance to negotiating these changes successfully.

The child's perspective

For children of divorcing families the threat of "rootlessness" is pervasive and looms large. A child wonders, and sometimes even asks, will I lose one or both of my parents, my grandparents, and the rest of the family? This fear of loss may be missed by child researchers, who are sometimes guided by their own values and fears and "tend to look over the heads of children into the eyes of adults."[6]

There is need, however, to further exploit both psychoanalytic development psychology and family systems theory in the light of what children are able to demonstrate to us about their feeling life. Children of divorce have usually, long before, experienced conflicts in the course of their own and their family's development. These conflicts may have been going on during their entire life span and therefore tend to antedate the divorce process by years. Developmental conflicts and feelings originating in the child's infancy and early years may be identified through their behavior. There may be physiological evidence of conflicts, as in infantile eczema or asthma, in children with a constitutional predisposition to these diseases. A young child not yet capable of verbal expression will reveal his or her conflicted feelings in play with family figures which are representative of mother, father, and siblings.

The feeling life of infants or young children include internalized representations of their caretakers and their conflicts about them. These, in turn, are significant to the development of their self, their self-image, and their behavior. According to Winicott,

> A child feels that things inside are good or bad, just as outside things are good or bad . . . The child's ability to keep alive what he loves and to retain his belief in his own love has an important bearing on how good or bad the things inside him and outside him feel to him to be; and this is to some extent true even of the infant of only a few months.[7]

The following example is a case in point:

> Tony and Mrs. Brown, his mother, were enrolled in an inner city therapeutic nursery. Tony's mother was a depressed young woman in her early twenties. Tony was two-and-a-half years old. When the child, fresh from exploration of his feelings in "family play," ran out of the nursery into the parents' room to his mother's side, he reached for her with both arms. Seated next to the social worker, her arms at her side, Mrs. Brown made no gesture towards Tony. This evidence of failure in the relationship between Tony and his mother became important in the assessment of his problems.
>
> Tony's mother and father met at a disco dance, a rare outing for her. Marriage followed and she became pregnant soon thereafter. In the meantime, Tony's father developed a severe bone injury and was no longer

able to work. Within months after Tony's birth, Mr. Brown left the family, and Mrs. Brown returned to the home where her mother, grandmother, and an older sister and her daughter lived. Mrs. Brown's only other sibling, a younger brother, had been "turned out" of this family because of aggressive behavior and minor infractions of the law. All of the males, the husbands and a son, had left this home within a period of eight years. The rest of the family, consisting of four generations of females and Tony, remained intact; its able women, other than Mrs. Brown, were employed in educational and welfare agencies.

At birth, Tony was named Alfred for his father. Whenever the change in Tony's name was brought up, Mrs. Brown showed her anger. During the three years that Tony was in the nursery, he visited his paternal grandmother, who called him "Al," about three or four times a year. His father also lived there. In play, Tony revealed to his teachers and therapist that he identified with both his father and his mother's mild-mannered boyfriend. His visits to his father, as well as his family plays that included an aggressive father, were followed by easily discernible aggressive play, both in the nursery and with his mother. Mrs. Brown responded to Tony's aggressive moods with anger and then punishment. Awakened one night by asthma during one of these visits, Tony was restored to his mother's loving care. Tony became aware that he was not permitted to identify with his father and that he could not have his name. The therapeutic nursery's clinical-educational team unfortunately had no access to Tony's father. When Tony was five and became ready for school, Mr. Brown remarried. Mrs. Brown forbade further contact between Mr. Brown and his son, and the effect of this loss on Tony was enormous.

The timing of the custody decision and the divorce of his parents appeared to be of little consequence to Tony

and his feeling responses as the divorce became final
when he was only six months old. But the ongoing
threat of being cut off from his father almost from birth
and the anger and withdrawal of his mother from him
were significant to Tony's feeling life, and affected his
physical health. His mother had gained full custody,
was the final arbiter of visitation rights, and she had cut
Tony off from his father completely.

Children's symptoms often mirror those in one or the other
parent, and parents themselves may repeat earlier developmental conflicts of their own in which the child becomes a "stand-
in" for an earlier actor or for the spouse. Benedek and Benedek
suggest that if the non-custodial parent is given access to the
child or children, he or she ". . . is afforded some opportunity to
rework his own developmental conflicts through parenthood."[8] This reworking may be of benefit to both parent and
child.

Children of divorce, like all children, have the right to be
"wanted." With ongoing contact, children are continually
aware of parental love in spite of parental anger and ambivalence. Lack of access to the non-custodial parent tends to produce in the child feelings of rejection by the absent parent as
well as feelings of being unloved and unwanted.

Divorce as warfare

What threatens in divorce is a kind of warfare between factions
which produces the opposite of access. The child may be a
hostage in the settlement of property rights; a spy for one side
against the other; a prisoner in one camp, prevented from
escape to the other; an unwilling or, if willing, an unsuited
ambassador from one side to the other. All these roles are
incompatible with his own healthy development, and he must
be protected from falling into them.

The problem is that the divorce process—the movements and statements of divorcing parents and their lawyers in contested cases—is more suited to warfare than to the promotion of child development. Much of what happens in the divorce process can be seen as the pre-emptive gaining of territory before the battle begins, with keeping up the morale of the troops, with propaganda and calculation about the motives of the enemy. All too often, the hostility of the client rubs off on the lawyer, and vice versa. It takes a conscious restructuring in the attitudes of all parties to bring about changes, especially in those cases where custody is contested in court. The actual moves in a hotly contested case—the efforts to assign blame or to prove one parent unfit, or the bargaining exchange of visitation for support—need to be reconsidered and recognized as elements that may thwart the child's eventual working through of the separation by the way they restrict access to both parents. The participation of an impartial mental health expert in the process, whether as child advocate or agent of the court, can provide the opportunity to construct occasions of understanding between family members.

The need for a new rite of passage

The battles of divorce and custody create an unprepared-for crisis of separation in the child's life. The circle of adults surrounding the child at that time—parents, extended family, lawyers, mental health experts, and judges—should work toward helping the child get through that crisis. This can be achieved through an artificial but very important group of meetings and other communications, a new and special rite of passage consciously designed to help the child move from being the child of a troubled family to being the child of two, perhaps less troubled, but certainly much less connected and accessible, family fragments.

There needs to be, from the child's point of view, not only a way of acknowledging his losses, but also a way of integrating what may later become gains. He now has a larger extended family. If everyone stays in contact, he has the possibility of seeing both parents in new contexts with new friends, perhaps with new partners. The ultimate goal, from the child's point of view, is turning these difficult facts of life into something as positive as possible. That is essentially what this report is about.

Relevant research and systematic investigations

Having reviewed the problem in theoretical terms, we now turn to the small body of clinical investigation and research that bears upon the question: What does happen to children of divorce when the custody is handled in one way or another? There is nothing in the literature that answers that question directly, but there are some studies that bear upon it indirectly. What follows is our resumé of the little evidence there is. Among others, we will consider:

- Michael Rutter's comprehensive epidemiological review[9] of maternal deprivation, which contains some evidence on parental separation relevant to our concerns.

- Wallerstein and Kelly's prospective clinical study[10-15] of children from the point of divorce to five years later, which supports many of our views on the importance of access.

- McDermott's study[16] of sixteen nursery school children during the immediate period of parental divorce, indicating that the divorce operates as an acute stress on the young child.

- A prospective comparision by Hetherington, Cox, and Cox[17] of divorced and non-divorced families, which contains some suggestive findings on the relationship between access and the adjustment of the child.

- A clinical study of selected cases by Tessman[18] on the later sequelae of unresolved parental separation, which illustrates the importance of access to the missing parent.

Studies of attachment and separation

This field is well reviewed by Michael Rutter in his book, THE QUALITY OF MOTHERING: MATERNAL DEPRIVATION REASSESSED.[19] As the title indicates, most work in this area focuses on the child's attachment to and separation from the mother, beginning with the work of John Bowlby and René Spitz. These investigators reported that deprivation of contact with a mothering person early in life, as in the case of infants reared in orphanages, can have serious and irreversible consequences for the child's later development. Their findings fit well the clinical experience of a child's immediate response to separation caused by illness, travel, death or divorce. The depression, anger, denial, and restorative attempts of children are clearly more painful and damaging than those of adults, at least in the short run.

Studies of the long-term consequences of separation are, however, more complicated, according to Rutter. The effects of separation are different at different ages of the child and are altered by the nature of both the previous and subsequent relationships. A separation is not merely an event that wounds the child's psyche, nor simply the defect of an object in the inner world; it is an event in a whole changing social web of which the child is a part. Thus, the consequences of separation due to death of a parent are often more benign than the consequences of divorce, presumably because the child has the support of other bereaved people in the family who can help him with his loss. Divorce or separation, on the other hand, often leads to no reconciliation of the loss. They may lead to nothing but fighting between two parents, each of whom is less available to the child. Similarly, the effect of any separation, for whatever reason, is greatly influenced by the quality of the relationships involved.

Summarizing follow-up studies of delinquency in children, Rutter says:

> Delinquency is thus associated with breaks— separation, divorces, desertions which follow parental discord, or discord without a break, but *not* with a break-up of the home as such. In fact, delinquency is *less* associated with parental death, with its necessary disruption of bonds, than it is with parental divorce, where bonds may still be maintained by intermittent contact after the break-up of the marriage. It may be concluded that it is distortion of relationships rather than bond disruption as such which causes the damage.[20]

On the positive side, the development of attachment, Rutter notes that children form many important bonds with many different people, and that these bonds serve different functions at different ages:

> Of course in most families the mother has most to do with the young child and as a consequence she is usually the person with whom the strongest bond is formed. But it should be appreciated that the chief bond need not be with a biological parent, it need not be with the chief caretaker, and it need not be with a female.
>
> Furthermore, it seems to be incorrect to regard the person with whom there is the main bond as necessarily and generally the most important person in the child's life. That person will be most important for some things but not for others. For some aspects of development the same-sexed parent seems to have a special role, for some the person who plays and talks most with the

child, and for others the person who feeds the child. The
father, the mother, brothers and sisters, friends, school-
teachers, and others all have an impact on development,
but their influence and importance differ for different
aspects of development.[21]

The child's loss of the father may be as injurious as the loss of
the mother. Kestenbaum and Stone[22] describe the responses of
thirteen girls who had lost their fathers: ". . . at some point
between infancy and adolescence . . . the missing father and the
girl's intense longing for the father were the key dynamic
issues." Lack of contact with the father promoted over-
idealization with marked hostility to the mother, or "a
reaction-formation against their hostility," accompanied by a
deepening of their dependency. Homosexuality was sometimes
a maladaptive response. When the mother's self-esteem was
low and she was depressed, the girls demonstrated a remarkable
need for the missing parent.[23]

Young parents today who are committed to sharing "natural
childbirth" and infant care tend to develop strong relationships with their infants. Mother and father, in these instances,
are both psychological parents; during the divorce process their
children feel keenly the loss of the non-custodial parent. The
Benedeks suggest that, when children of divorce are of pre-
school age, fantasied images of the absent father may haunt the
child for life, particularly those of the parent of the opposite
sex. They believe that access to the non-custodial parent ". . .
provides an avenue by which the child can test the reality of
images which are a product of his own fantasies and the impressions of others that have been communicated to him."[24]

Studies of the children of divorce

We now turn to the small but extremely significant body of
systematic studies which bear on this question.

Wallerstein and Kelly[25] have addressed themselves to investigating what happens to previously well-adjusted children when their parents are divorced, based on the experiences of a Marin County, California, clinic. By offering counseling to the children of divorcing families, they were able to examine carefully 131 children, ranging in age from two-and-a-half to eighteen, and to compare their adjustment at the time of divorce, one year later, and then five years later. They used interviews with the children, their parents, teachers, and others. Prior to the divorce, the children had had no history of psychological difficulty, they were doing well at school, and they were developing on schedule. This population came from an area where relatively stable, middle-class life is the common experience, so that the findings were not confounded with the effects of poverty, crime and social breakdown.

The children were separated into pre-school, early and late latency, and adolescent groups, since the effect in each age group was different. In the aggregate, however, these reports make clear that, for almost all of these well-adjusted children, the emotional consequences of divorce were bitterly painful, and for the time period studied, the effects quite adverse. The data give no support to the common idea that children of unhappy families are better off after divorce has parted their quarreling parents, certainly not immediately afterwards.

It appears that, a year later, the children of different ages had different kinds and degrees of difficulty, and the authors define several features of post-divorce accommodation that appear to be important. Significant features were part of the *process* of change in the relationships over time. The degree of distress at the first interview, that is, at the time of divorce, did not predict later developments. The worst effects in terms of the children's symptoms and developmental retardation were correlated with continued conflict and blame between the divorcing parents, and with lack of access to the absent parent.

In the pre-school children, for example, trouble was related to the breakdown of the custodial parent's resources (usually the mother's). The nature of the mother's relationship with the child changed in ways impossible to foresee from an evaluation of the situtation before divorce. In every case, the ties with the fathers of these young children remained strong; the fathers stuck to their children despite obstacles put up by the mothers. For children *of this age,* continued good relations with the absent fathers did not prevent the general downhill course seen in 44 percent of these cases. They appeared to be "in significantly worsened psychological condition" in one year's time at the second checkpoint of the study. Initial regression was the rule in the two-and-a-half to three-and-one-quarter year old group. The initial symptoms were not related to the "number of symptoms demonstrated . . . by the child or psychological health or developmental progress of the child a year later. . ." The relevant variable was the quality of the caretaking assumed by the mother, father, or a substitute caretaker employed by the primary parent. Wallerstein and Kelly also noted that, for the youngest pre-school children in the first year of divorce, when "the intensity of the divorce discord had remained relatively undiminished . . . a tender attachment between the child and the departing father may render the child more vulnerable to the mother's unremitted anger." In the middle pre-school group, ages three-and-three-quarters to four-and-three quarters, "their concept of the dependability of human relationships and of object ties was profoundly shaken and they were frightened, confused, and sad."[26]

The above findings seem to be in agreement with McDermott's earlier study[27] of sixteen nursery school children, based on observations of their behavior by nursery school teachers. The behavior of three children—19 percent—seemed not to change, and it was noted that they were on good terms with each parent following the divorce. The majority of children, however, ten out of the sixteen—or 62 percent—showed dramatic changes in behavior, generally characterized by anxiety and depression and difficulty in mastering these feelings through play. The other three children—19 percent—showed less dramatic changes in their behavior, but tended to react in pseudo-adult ways that signaled future difficulty. However, the majority of children who showed regressive behavioral changes were able to improve and show signs of resolution and mastery both verbally and in play.

Wallerstein and Kelly's oldest pre-school group, "seemed to have a reasonable understanding of the divorce related changes . . . and were in no way impeded in their developmental progress." In this oldest group, however, there were more troubled girls than boys with "prolonged investment in oedipal fantasies, diminished self-esteem, and delayed entry into latency . . ."[28]

For latency children (over five), especially for boys, contact with fathers was very important. Of a sample of children in early latency, only two out of twenty-six had "stopped visiting their fathers of their own accord, without evidence of anger. In each case, the mother had remarried and the new step-parent was providing unaccustomed gratification to these children."[29] Other children in this age group were urgently requesting that their mothers remarry. The typical every-two-week contact with fathers was not enough for most children. The boys who were really satisfied were those able to see their fathers at any time, for instance, by biking over to his new residence whenever they wanted to.

In early latency, the children's "awareness of the realities of divorce," combined with immature ego structures, made for difficulty in integrating the painful experience. Anxiety was intense with the necessity of denial.[30] The later latency children, however, showed various efforts to manage "by seeking coherence, by denial, by courage, by bravado, by seeking support from others, by conscious avoidance . . . All emerged as age-available ways of coping with the profound feelings of loss and rejection, of helplessness and loneliness . . ." As compared with younger children, their more sophisticated and mature grasp of time and reality and history increased their comprehension of the meanings and consequences of divorce . . .," while enabling them better to temper the impact.[31]

One boy of nine manipulated his divorced parents into acting as if they were married at his parents' night at school, although he did not trust them to get married again "since the same thing would happen if they did." A girl of ten developed an active fantasy life using transitional objects such as a panda bear, or even a pencil, which protected her from feelings of rejection by the parents. "The single feeling that most clearly distinguished this group from all younger children was their conscious intense anger. . ." Increased aggressiveness and identification with the father, little guilt or feeling of responsibility for the divorce, a shaken sense of identity, and threats to socialization and superego formation were all observed.[32.]

Wallerstein and Kelly feel that family disruption "poses a very specific hazard" to the normal adolescent process of emancipation from primary love objects, but if the disruption does not come prematurely, that is, prior to normal detachment, it may indeed even facilitate the road to independence and maturity. The adolescent may be able to "transform feelings of helplessness into a sense of control via active mastery." Depressions, rages, and sexual impulses may be troublesome, the last in relation to "revivified oedipal impulses"; also, "feelings of loss, emptiness, and loneliness [are] much exacerbated." Adolescents who did best were those able to gain some distance from the parental conflict and were able to make a more or less objective assessment of how each of their parents was behaving. This required continuous access and an absence of involvement in the mutual blaming of the parents.[33] Certain conclusions stand out at the five-year mark.[34] Wallerstein and Kelly found a close correlation between continued contact with the non-custodial parent and the child's self-esteem. This connection was especially strong among the older youngsters, particularly the boys. Conversely, they found a significant link between depression in children at the five-year mark and disrupted or much impoverished contact with the non-custodial parent. This link did not hold when the non-custodial parent was psychiatrically disturbed. It was as if the loss were less.

There was an interesting finding about the anger of children in the nine to twelve-year-old age group which has implications about children being consulted regarding their choice of custodial parent.

> The longlasting anger of children in . . . [this] . . . group at the parent whom they held responsible for the divorce, the eagerness of these youngsters to be co-opted into the parental battling, their willingness to take sides, often against a parent to whom they had been tenderly attached during the intact marriage, the intense compassionate caretaking relations which led some of these youngsters to rescue a distressed parent, often to their own detriment, have led us to rethink our expectations of these children. We doubt their capacity to make informed judgment about plans which would be in their own best interest.[35]

They conclude that

> The relationship between the child of divorce and both of the original parents did not diminish in emotional importance to the child over the five years within the post-divorce family. Although the mother's caretaking and psychological role became increasingly central in these families, the father's psychological significance did not correspondingly decline.[36]

They also took a clear position in favor of continuity with both parents, stating,

> Taken as a whole, our findings point to the desirability of the child's continuing the relationship with both parents during the post-divorce years in an arrangement which enables each parent to be responsible for and genuinely concerned about the well-being of the children . . . Put simply, the central hazard which divorce poses to the psychological health and development of children and adolescents is in the diminished or disrupted parenting which so often follows in the wake of the rupture and which can become consolidated within the post-divorce family.[37]

Hetherington, Cox and Cox[38] have provided the only detailed epidemiological study of the behavior of divorced parents and its effects on relations with children. They studied ninety-six families divided into black/white, divorced/not divorced groups. Their measures included interviews, structured diary records, home, school and laboratory observation of interactions, teacher ratings and others, taken at two months, one year, and two years following divorce.

Concerning visitation, they found:

> When there was agreement in child rearing, a positive attitude toward the spouse, low conflict between the divorced parents, and when the father was emotionally mature . . . the frequency of father's contact with the child was associated with more positive mother-child interactions. When there was disagreement and inconsistency in attitudes toward the child, and conflict and ill will between the divorced parents, or when the father was poorly adjusted, frequent visitation was associated with poor mother-child functioning and disruptions in the children's behavior. Emotional maturity in the mother was also found to be related to her adequacy in

coping with stresses in her new single life and relations
with children.

Other support systems such as that of grandparents,
brothers and sisters, close friends, or a competent
housekeeper also were related to the mother's effective-
ness in interacting with the child in divorced but not
intact families. However, they were not as salient as a
continued positive relationship of the ex-husband with
the family.[39]

It is not clear from their results, however, how frequently the
adverse condition was found. In fact, since the sample was not
drawn randomly from a population of divorcing parents, and
since there was considerable sample attrition, an estimate of
true frequency of nonworkable situations could not have been
derived. But the relationships described above exist, at least in
this group.

The investigations described so far do not really test the
clinician's idea that there is a long-term psychological risk
involved in serving a parental relationship even when it is the
source of difficulty for the child. What actually happens to such
cut-off relationships, especially with parents who are regarded
ambivalently, is the subject of a clinical study by Tessman.
Reviewing fifty psychotherapy cases, she finds that older children and young adults are often involved in an unwitting quest
for that absent parent. This quest may, in the case of young
adults, lead to troubles within the close relationships they
choose to form. Tessman concludes:

> For the children of the divorced, continued reality
> testing was usually possible to greater or lesser extent.
> Input derived from continued contacts about what the
> parent was really like could help transform the magical
> images of childhood to both less fearsome and less
> magnetic proportions. This process was not available
> to some, either because of the withdrawal of the absent

parent or the hostility of the remaining one. It seemed particularly difficult in some of the cases in which divorce coincided not only with the pubescence of the child, but also with the devaluation of the parent in the human support network surrounding the child.[40]

Response to Goldstein, Freud, and Solnit*

The proposals advanced in their work[41] appear valid, as they apply to adoption and foster care, and their case examples buttress their conclusions. The extension and extrapolation, however, to custody disputes in divorce is not validated. While we agree that speed is important in determining custody and that a minimum of litigation is desirable, our disagreements with these authors are basic.

Goldstein, Freud and Solnit have based their conclusions on several major supports. The first is the concept that the child has a single psychological parent—a view which derives from the psychoanalytic theory of object constancy. We noted above that the empirical work which has been both carried out and reviewed by Rutter demonstrates that the child from early infancy can and often does have more than one psychological parent. In fact, it is usual for children of toddler age and beyond to have multiple attachments—to parents, grandparents, siblings, extended family members and other caregivers. What matters is the genuineness and the constancy of the care. The importance of object constancy may be valid if the object is viewed as the family or system of caregivers, but not if the caretaking has to be limited to a single person.

---

* Editor's Note: The 1979 edition of BEYOND THE BEST INTERESTS OF THE CHILD includes an Epilogue in which the authors take into consideration some of the critical comments which were made following publication of their work in 1973. Specifically they address two of the issues which suggested to them the need for clarification of the least detrimental alternative standard, particularly as it applies to disposition decisions.

What these authors do not recognize is that, in these disputes, we are usually dealing with two psychological parents, a mother and a father. The research cited above, particularly the Wallerstein-Kelly studies, demonstrate the adverse effects of cutting the child off from one of his or her psychological parents. The child needs both parents.

Secondly, the proposal that the custodial parent determine the contact of the child with the other parent fails to take into account the fact that the child has a right as well as a need for contact with both parents. Parents may divorce each other for their own reasons, but in that process, they do not have the right to force their children to divorce the other parent.

Thirdly, the assumption that, once a custody decision has been made, courts should not intervene except in cases of neglect or abandonment, does not take into account the fact that the children of divorce are children "at risk" and that society has a legitimate concern about their welfare and development.

Conclusion

The evidence and our own experience lead us to what can be called the family perspective on divorce and custody. Briefly, that perspective rests on the following concepts. A couple that comes together to form a family and raise children creates for those children something that is more than the sum of its parts—more than the dyadic relations one-on-one with mother and separately with father. We find no evidence for the existence of a single "psychological parent" with whom the tie is critically more important than with the rest of the network.

The relationships with mother and father, and with grandparents and others as well, constitute an emotional universe that, especially in the early years, forms a pattern for the child's later relations. If, in the crisis of divorce, one part of that universe is cut off, labeled as bad, and becomes unavailable, there will be adverse consequences for the child's view of himself and of the people he will relate to later in life.

Even if the person who is cut off is a very ambivalently held parent with whom contact is difficult and painful, our experience and the evidence convince us that the later ability to put that relationship in emotional perspective is better served through contact than through separation.

REFERENCES

1. E. H. Erikson, "Ego Development and Historical Change," in IDENTITY AND THE LIFE CYCLE (Vol. 1, No. 1 in the Psychological Issues Series) (New York: International Universities Press, 1959) pp 18-49.

2. John Bowlby, ATTACHMENT AND LOSS (New York: Basic Books, 1969).

3. Michael Rutter, THE QUALITY OF MOTHERING: MATERNAL DEPRIVATION REASSESSED (Hammondsworth, England: Penguin Books, 1974).

4. Bruce Dohrenwend and J. M. de Figuerido, "Remote and Recent Life Events and Psychopathology," in PREVENTION OF MENTAL ILLNESS, RESEARCH FRONTIERS, Ricks, Dohrenwend, and Langsley, eds [forthcoming].

5. G. Brown and T. Harris, THE SOCIAL ORIGINS OF DEPRESSION (London: Tavistock, 1978).

6. S. L. Lightfoot, A CHILD'S PLACE: TOWARD A MORE COMPLEX VIEW, IRCD Bulletin, a Publication of the Institute for Urban and Minority Education, Teachers College, Columbia University, 1976.

7. D. W. Winicott, THROUGH PEDIATRICS TO PSYCHOANALYSIS (New York: Basic Books, 1975).

8. R. S. Benedek and E. P. Benedek, Postdivorce Visitation: A Child's Right, *Journal of Child Psychiatry* 16,2 (1977) 256-271.

9. See note 3.

10. J. Wallerstein and J. Kelly, The Effects of Parental Divorce: Experiences of the Pre-School Child, *Journal of American Academy of Child Psychiatry* 1414 (1975) 600-616.

11. _____ , The Effects of Parental Divorce: Experiences of the Child in Early Latency, *American Journal of Orthopsychiatry* 46,1 (1976) 20-32.

12. _____ , The Effects of Parental Divorce: Experiences of the Child in Later Latency, *American Journal of Orthopsychiatry* 46,2 (1976) 256-269.

13. _____ , The Effects of Parental Divorce: The Adolescent Experience, in THE CHILD IN HIS FAMILY: CHILDREN AT A PSYCHIATRIC RISK, Vol. 3 E. J. Anthony and C. Koupernik, eds (New York: John Wiley and Sons, 1974) pp 479-506.

14. _____ , Divorce Counseling: A Community Service for Families in the Midst of Divorce, *American Journal of Orthopsychiatry*, 47,1 (1977) 4-22.

15. _____ , Brief Interventions with Children in Divorcing Families, *American Journal of Orthopsychiatry* 47,1 (1977) 23-29.

16. J. F. McDermott, Parental Divorce in Early Childhood, *American Journal of Psychiatry* 124,10 (1968) 1424-1432.

17. E. M. Hetherington, M. Cox and R. Cox, "Beyond Father Absence: Conceptualization of Effects of Divorce," in CONTEMPORARY READINGS IN CHILD PSYCHOLOGY, E. M. Hetherington & R. Parke, eds (New York: McGraw Hill, 1977).

18. L. H. Tessman, "The Quest for the Wanted Absent Parent in Children of the·Divorced and Deceased," paper presented at the meeting of the American Orthopsychiatric Association, Spring 1977.

19. See note 3.

20. Ibid., p 108.

21. Ibid., p 125.

22. C. J. Kestenbaum and M. H. Stone, The Effects of Fatherless Homes Upon Daughters: Clinical Impressions Regarding Paternal Deprivation, *Journal of the American Academy of Psychoanalysis*, 4,2 (1976) 71-190.

23. Ibid., p 182.

24. See note 8, p 261.

25. See notes 10 through 15.

26. See note 10.

27. See note 16.

28. See note 10.

29. See note 11.

30. Ibid.

31. See note 12.

32. Ibid.

33. See note 13.

34. J. S. Wallerstein and J. B. Kelly, SURVIVING THE BREAKUP (New York: Basic Books, 1980).

35. Ibid., p 314.

36. Ibid.

37. Ibid., p 310.

38. See note 17.

39. Ibid., p 314.

40. See note 18, p 20.

41. J. Goldstein, Anna Freud, and A. J. Solnit, BEYOND THE BEST INTERESTS OF THE CHILD (New York: The Free Press, 1973).

4

THE FAMILY APPROACH TO
CHILD CUSTODY DETERMINATIONS

As described in Chapter 3 an adequate custody decision requires an evaluation of the total family and its relationships. No *single* principle or finding concerning an individual family member can determine a "best" resolution to a custody conflict, since that principle or finding generally turns out to be only a part of the matrix of the whole family. Perhaps the following case vignette will illustrate how custody decisions look differently when viewed from individual and family perspectives.

Alice B was thirteen when her recently divorced mother came for consultation because of her concern for Alice's health and safety. Alice was considered a "bright, normal child," who had grown up in a middle-class family and neighborhood. She had many friends and did well in school. Her father was described as a "self-centered" executive who was not very available to Alice or to her ten-year-old brother. Mrs. B was a housewife who had married her husband just after her graduation from high school.

Mr. and Mrs. B had begun having marital difficulties about five years before the consultation, when Alice was about eight. Initially the arguments stemmed from Mr. B's frequent absences on business assignments. Their problems grew more serious over the next two years, and Mr. and Mrs. B sought marriage counseling. The couple were unsuccessful in their attempt to reconcile their difficulties. At about that time, when Alice was ten, she began to show evidence of serious behavioral problems, including fighting with peers, drug abuse, drinking, and school delinquency.

When Mr. and Mrs. B finally decided to divorce, Mr. B moved into an apartment. Alice began to live with her father after he had suggested to Mrs. B that she was the cause of Alice's difficulties. He felt that she would do better if she left her mother. Mrs. B allowed Mr. B to have custody of Alice, and she obtained custody of their son.

After the custody settlement, Alice's behavioral problems escalated. She ran away from school and was increasingly provocative as Mr. B was less available. Alice continued to use drugs and to have sexual relationships with older men. After each such episode, Alice would contact her mother, tell her what she, Alice, had been doing, and would ask Mrs. B to bring her home. Mrs. B would comply and return Alice to her father. Then Alice would run away again. Mr. B refused to participate more actively in Alice's care or to allow Mrs. B or the state to take custody.

It seems apparent that Alice was experiencing great anguish, and that her acting-out behavior was her way of expressing her distress. Her mother's projected sense of inadequacy and her father's detachment left the child with a decreased sense of self esteem. She felt abandoned and unwanted, and her behavior seemed calculated to get care and attention.

The marital problems represented a turning point for this family; they were followed by an escalation of difficulties that became more pronounced when the custody decision was made. A careful evaluation at that time with clear definitions of parental responsibilities, expectations, and resources might have made an important difference. Of the parents, Mrs. B demonstrated more investment and concern about her daughter's well-being and appears to have been the more stable and consistent. Alice was asking for her support and closeness, although she was not able to ask for these directly. Mr. B, though he wanted custody of Alice, never demonstrated the capacity to be a caring, available parent. Yet Mrs. B, because she felt guilty about her daughter's difficulties, allowed him to have custody of Alice. This inappropriate arrangement gave Mr. B the opportunity to express his anger with his wife and reinforced Mrs. B's sense of guilt and failure.

In this case, the family approach would look at the quality of the relationship between the children and both of the parents and assess the interactions among them, rather than allow an unwise agreement—based on one parent's judgment—to control the situation. It is obvious that that basis for a custody decision did not bring results that served the best interests of Alice or of the family.

On the other hand, some of the more familiar considerations in custody evaluations that appear to focus primarily on the individual, prove, on closer scrutiny, to illustrate principles of family interaction. For example, there is wide agreement on the value of maintaining continuity of school, neighborhood, and friendships for children involved in a custody conflict, and on preserving the integrity of sibling relationships. But guidelines function only when viewed comparatively, and in the context of the relative stability of the different family units created by the divorce. Further, it requires little sophistication in human relationships to recognize that it is impossible to evaluate families adequately simply on the basis of external criteria, such as an affluent home, nourishing food, or the prospect of inheriting money. The quality of the family which supplies such resources is critically important.

The weighing of all these conflicting values and priorities can be brought together in terms of "best interests," as the

Benedeks discuss in commenting on the Michigan law,[1] but
that in turn should be aimed at the decision *least destructive to
the entire family interaction*. In other words, there can be a
number of different solutions which might be considered to
serve the "best interests" of the child, but these different solutions need to be compared in terms of the total family interaction because the child will continue to relate to both parents
and their families of origin. The child's need for access to his
now-severed family is crucial.

We propose, from the perspective of family psychiatry, five
broad guidelines that should be recognized and carefully
weighed in determining a custody decision.

1. Custody decisions should be part of the process of devel-
opmental change in a family.

While parents may achieve a legal divorce from each other, they
cannot divorce themselves from their children or their responsibilities to them. Continued contact between all individuals in
the family should be expected over an extended period of time.
A mutually acceptable compromise by contesting parties, as
opposed to a "knuckling under" by one of them, can facilitate
future constructive interactions and minimize the hostility and
acrimony that so often occur in the post-divorce discussions
about the children. In this context, the use of a custody demand
as a *quid pro quo* for a better financial arrangement is to be
deplored. Such an approach treats the children as mere chattels
or weapons and makes a genuine compromise more difficult to
achieve.

Process resolutions of custody conflicts—those reached by
the parents themselves through a process of negotiation—have
the advantage of encouraging parental responsibility for children. The ease of divorce in our time and the ready assumption
of public responsibility for children can permit parents to

become less responsible. We believe that a societal attitude, and a consequent judicial attitude, that focused less on parental rights to custody and visitation and more on parental responsibilities and on the rights of children to have access to both parents would promote more constructive custody decisions. Clinical experience with parents struggling with the guilt feelings attendant on divorce suggests that often parents who appear initially to be irresponsible can be encouraged to take a more responsible posture. It is important to assume that parents can and want to be responsible, even though they may not have been able to be so within the marriage.

The family is not a static system fixed forever at the point of a custody decision; nor can the course of its future development be accurately predicted. Subsequent events may weaken or fragment that part of the family that initially appeared the more stable, or circumstances may change in ways that could not have been foreseen. For example, the remarriage of a parent may completely alter the conditions under which custody was initially awarded. Generally, the more cooperative the negotiation between parents at the time of the custody decision, the better the chances for constructive renegotiation as circumstances change.

It is often assumed that, when one parent remarries, a new home will provide a replacement for the lost parent and is, therefore, desirable. This assumption ignores the conflicts in loyalties that may be engendered in the child, the problem of resolving his fantasy that his parents may be ultimately reunited, and the realities of the newly created family. The new home may well be desirable, but not because it replaces a lost parent.

In general, courts have agreed to grant reviews of custody decisions in response to the claim of changed circumstances. Justice Heffernan of the Superior Court of Wisconsin noted, in a 1966 case:

> It is fundamental in the law concerning the custody
> of children that the court retains jurisdiction, knowing
> full well that circumstances are likely to change and
> that new arrangements may therefore be necessary.[2]

The court has a role to play not only in the initial custody determination but also in the re-examination of such arrangements as they affect the substantive aspects of children's lives. Although we believe that court intrusion should be minimal, we feel that court actions can be reduced only as they are made unnecessary because contestants assume mutual responsibility for the care of their children. The continuity of a child's emotional relationships is of the utmost importance, and the consequences of disruption of that continuity must be considered. The possible development of feelings of abandonment, inability to trust, difficulty of forming deep relationships, and the potential for antisocial behavior have to be weighed against the other variables in the situation.

2. Family ties and family continuity have an importance that transcends divorce.

It has long been recognized that individual identity has its roots in family identity. Children who are separated from family members maintain active contact with them in fantasy, if not in reality. Ties and loyalties, sometimes invisible or covert, play a role in maintaining behavior towards other family members and outsiders. Understanding one's origins and having a sense of place within a family's history can help a child withstand the anguish of separation. Insofar as possible, custody determinations should provide access to both parents, and, in turn, to both sets of grandparents and other family members. In the situation where both parents are equally adequate, but are unable to work out an agreement on custody, the custody preferentially should be assigned to the one who is the more likely to provide such access.

The importance of intergenerational continuity may be well illustrated by the following case example:

> A five-year-old boy, after the funeral of his grandfather, began to search through family albums collecting all available photographs of his ancestors and to question all family members about them. After several months, he began to study the monarchy of the European country from which his grandparents had emigrated. It seems clear that he was attempting to resolve his grief over the loss of his grandfather through probing his family's origins and feeling more closely a part of their history.

Intergenerational continuity also implies contact with themes and values prevalent in the family. The severance of family ties may disrupt the process of integration into a family and alter the process of eventual separation and the child's own sense of individuality as it evolves in adolescence. Even where "objective" evidence of one parent's inappropriate behavior toward the child can be presented, it may be better for the child's development to allow an ongoing relationship in order to work through the ambivalence toward such a parent, unless there is a risk to the child's safety. Basic loyalties are not determined by judicial decisions. The child should be afforded an opportunity to work out his/her relationship, even with a parent who has behaved "inappropriately." Thus, it is of questionable merit to give one parent total control over access to the other parent and the extended family.

The principle supporting the need for a relationship with one parent should not, by itself, override the principle of intergenerational continuity, especially in view of the fact that the requirement for emotional closeness with a primary caretaker changes with the child's development. Further, to see the child solely as the recipient of care, attention, and affection is a perspective that overlooks the reciprocity in the parent-child relationship. Consider the example of the child who saw the impact of her father's violent behavior prior to the divorce, but who said thoughtfully, "maybe when we go visit Dad, if we keep him company, he will lose his violence."[3] We would urge an awareness of the child's concern for the parent's welfare, even when that parent seems to fail by ordinary social criteria. Without such awareness, the law, in its concern for protecting the child, may in fact make the child pay the heaviest price.

Providing access to both parents helps both child and parents deal with feelings that are evoked if the child looks like, is named for, or reminds the custodial parent of the divorced spouse. Since the divorced spouse has been rejected, the child may be vulnerable to anxieties about being abandoned or rejected himself. If, however, the non-custodial parent is accessible, the child will benefit from that parent's support and the consequent affirmation of his own identity.

The values that come from the child's having access to the love and care of both parents make divided or joint custody attractive options for consideration in some cases. The difficulties the parents have in their relationships with each other can provide a potential for growth in the child, if their differences do not jeopardize their love for him/her, and the child can recognize that. In addition, as previously noted, there is evidence that early loss of a parent correlates with the incidence of depression later in life.[4] It is worthwhile to strive for a custody determination that circumvents this sense of "loss" by keeping both parents within the child's milieu.

To quote from the Group for the Advancement of Psychiatry's report on parenthood:

> Despite the fact that one parent can rear children and meet their physical needs, children need two parents for complete psychological growth and development. What this means is that, in order for the child to concep-

tualize himself as a developing person, he must identify himself with two parents—a man and a woman, a father and a mother. If he is exposed to only one parent in his day-to-day living, he will inevitably invent the other in his mind. He will ask many questions, will try in all ways to get some feeling and information about his absent father or mother. If this is not forthcoming, he will in his fantasy create the parent he needs in order to feel good about himself as a person. If parents have not resolved their own feelings about each other, this process in the child will reawaken old feelings, angers, regrets, longings and whatever else is still there.

Children need some positive information about both parents and about the attitudes of the parents toward them and to each other. For purposes of building their own sense of self and self-respect, they need to know the assets and good qualities of each of their parents as well as those facts that led to ways in which their parents have failed them. They want to know what attracted the parents to each other, what each liked in the other. And although their larger understanding of why the parents separated will come as they become older, children have a need to know why their parents were divorced.

Consider the example of a nine-year-old boy whose divorced father is living away from home. He sees his father fairly regularly and likes many things about him. If he feels that his mother has strong feelings of rejection for his father and feels only negatively about him, he may have difficulty in identifying with his father. As a boy, he needs to like his father in some ways, but if he feels his mother totally rejects his father, he may begin to feel that his mother cannot really accept him either. Since he likes his mother and is dependent upon her for affection and acceptance he finds himself in conflict about his loyalties.[5]

It is sometimes supposed that an interested and sympathetic stepparent can replace the child's non-custodial parent and therefore obviate the need for contact with that parent. While acknowledging the substantial role that stepparents may play in the emotional development of children, we wish to emphasize that a child's loyalties to a stepparent and to a natural parent are different and separate. The presence of a stepparent should in no way be viewed as eliminating the need for the child's access to both his/her natural parents.

In emphasizing the importance of visitation by the non-custodial parent, it is useful to comment on the nature of that visitation. Often the non-custodial parent sees the child during a prearranged and generally short period of time; thus an ongoing responsible parenting role is not assumed by the non-custodial parent. The child is denied an opportunity to see the non-custodial parent in daily routines, while the custodial parent is seen in a variety of situations, including fatigue, irritability, and preoccupation with problems. Visiting arrangements that provide a better balance will enhance the child's perspective and facilitate the development of a more realistically based relationship. This requires planning time, space, and activities that foster the maintenance of the relationship between parent and child. A situation to be avoided is one like that of the father of a five-year-old boy, who found it necessary to fly to another city to see his son in museums, restaurants, and other public places because the court had restricted his visitation to short periods of time and had not allowed him to take the child to his own home.

There is no one overriding quality or competence that defines good or bad parenting. Competence in parenting represents a range of capabilities; there is no single, absolute trait against which contestants for custody can be evaluated. In our experience, for example, a parent who cannot *accept* love from a child may be as detrimental to the child's development as one who cannot *give* love.

3. The history of mental illness in a parent does not in itself, preclude effective parenting.

Custody awards made on the basis that one parent is "unfit" have derived in part from the diagnosis of psychiatric problems in the "unfit" parent. We frequently observe, however, that the family member initially referred for psychiatric help is not necessarily the "sickest" family member, but is, instead, part of a complex interactional system. A judgment concerning the unfitness of one parent in isolation from the context of the whole family is a fragmentary and possibly unreliable judgment. Frequently, what is seen as ill or pathological behavior is determined by the nature of the repeated interactions in a family. Individually or in another situation, the "sick" member may not exhibit the same maladaptive behavior. Furthermore, a judgment made on the basis of a present or past diagnosis of mental illness does not by itself establish the bearer as an unfit custodian of the child. The issue is how the emotional disturbance affects the interaction with the child.

While the award of custody should not automatically be made against the parent with a mental illness, it should not be made solely because the child can be demonstrated to support the mental health or welfare of one parent. Also, it should be noted that a kind of "Gresham's Law" tends to operate in these situations over time: the more healthy parent tends to give in to the less healthy one; the more flexible parent to the more rigid one; the one who wants the divorce more urgently, to the one who is not immediately eager.[6] It is important, therefore, that there be some monitoring during the negotiation so that distorted compromises between parents and the use of the child as a pawn can be averted.

4. **Prevailing values regarding family styles do not necessarily correlate with parenting capabilities.**

One risk inherent in the principle of denying custody to "unfit" parents is that social judgments about values and lifestyle often enter into assessments and decisions. Thus, in the recent past (and perhaps even currently), women were seen as inherently more able than men to parent young children. This view has become questionable, and alternative custody arrangements have sometimes been made, as in the case of the R family which follows:

> Mr. and Mrs. R, both in their late thirties, had marital difficulties. Mrs. R felt that Mr. R did not take her wishes into account, and Mr. R felt that Mrs. R was not interested in him or in their son, now aged five, but had married him only because he was wealthy. During the year after they separated, he learned that she was leaving the care of the boy to his step-sister, aged eleven, and to a maid, while she worked days and went out nights and weekends. When she sent the boy away to overnight camp, despite his protests, Mr. R filed suit for custody. An evaluation was conducted and the recommendation was that Mr. R have custody of the child. Mr. R was seen as a more devoted parent who was prepared to interact with his son and spend more quality time with him.

Another aspect of this problem of conflicting values is the large number of people with alternative lifestyles who are parents. The current landscape is dotted with experimental social units—communal "families," homosexual "families," single-parent "families," all of which have been perceived by some as unsatisfactory arrangements for children, although their effects upon normal child development cannot be assessed with certainty. Evidence suggests that a lack of love and attention, rather than specific arrangements are more critical for the child. The identification of one contestant in a custody dispute with an unusual style of family or community life or a different religious practice cannot be assumed in itself to establish his or her unfitness. Furthermore, society's standards change constantly. The presence of any single behavioral factor such as alcoholism, unconventional sexual habits, lack of incentive for education, or behavior that irritates the neighbors, does not, in isolation, determine the quality of the parenting relationship. While it might be better for the child to be exposed to parents who espouse normative values and behaviors, an alternative life style can be weighed only as part of the whole family's situation. The M family provides a case in point.

> Mr. and Mrs. M have been separated for one year and are in the process of obtaining a divorce. They have two children, a daughter aged ten, and a son aged eight. The children have been living with Mrs. M and her lesbian friend since the separation. Recently, Mrs. M's homosexuality was disclosed. Mr. M wants custody of the children. There has been no evidence that the children are neglected or disturbed, and they have a warm and caring relationship with their mother. Mrs. M wants to retain custody, and she actively supports the children's desires to see and relate to their father. Mr. M feels that Mrs. M's homosexuality is dangerous to the children's well-being and he does not want them to see her.

From one perspective, homosexuality could be weighed as a major detriment and Mrs. M would be considered unfit. From a family perspective, however, the need for maintaining contact with both parents is a more important priority for the children's future development, as long as there is no evidence that the mother is denigrating men in general and the father in particular. Furthermore, since there is a good relationship between Mrs. M and the children, the effect of disrupting that relationship would be damaging to them.

5. A child's opinion in custody disputes has relevance, but it is only one part of the evaluation and should not alone determine custody.

The practice of leaving custody decisions up to the child, or of making the decision appear to stem from the child's preference, places the child in a situation of conflicting loyalties.

The child, in an attempt to deal with the guilt, anger, and fear of being abandoned or rejected, as well as with the sadness at the loss of the family as it had been, may respond in a variety of ways. He/she may become angry at the parent seen as responsible for the divorce, and may reject that parent, in spite of an otherwise good relationship. He/she may invite punishment and attempt restitution and expiation by submitting to the stronger parent. He/she may withdraw or become self-destructive, or make a masochistic choice. In addition, different children in the same family may have different views, depending on age, sex, developmental state, and personal idiosyncrasies. To force the child to make a decision engenders guilt. It may also prematurely induce separation conflicts at a time that is developmentally inappropriate. The perceptions and wishes of the child should certainly be taken into account, but, if the child does indicate a preference, the decision—whether by parents or the court—should be interpreted to the child as based upon many considerations, only one of which is his own stated preference. A child's immediate preference may not accord with his own long-term well-being, as the case of the T family demonstrates.

> Mr. T had not seen his son for five years after his divorce from Mrs. T, but when she became ill, he agreed to take Tony, aged seven, for the Christmas holidays. While the boy was visiting, Mr. T decided to request custody. Tony was delighted because his father had bought him many presents; he had fewer material possessions at home because his mother could not afford them.

In this case, the court wisely sought consultation with a mental health professional who, in addition to pointing out that there was no reason for a change, also remarked on the longstanding caring relationship Tony had with his mother and to the potential damage attendant upon losing that. Tony had idealized his absent father, perhaps partly to deny his own feelings of rejection.

Civil codes in some states mandate that, unless the parent selected by the child is judged unfit, the choice of a child of defined age (see Chapter 2) is to be honored. The courts have, in some instances, recognized the potential hazards of this practice. Justice Crockett[7] of the Utah Appeals Court, for example, dissented from a custody determination by the children of a divorced couple:

> If the mere fact that a child has become ten years old endows him with power to make a choice of his parental custodian, which must be honored in any event, and whether his reasons are good or bad, or in fact whether he has any reasons at all, so that his choice is absolute and not subject to control or review by anyone, even by the court, he could be empowered to make a decision of the gravest possible consequence to himself, his family, and society, under circumstances where, because of his immaturity, and the usual emotional stress, there is little assurance that his judgment would be sound. It would be one of the most arbitrary and far-reaching prerogatives known to the law. This is plainly nonsensical and impractical.

Conclusion

A family perspective on child custody emphasizes the continuity and mutuality of family relationships and responsibilities, despite divorce. To some extent, the family continues to exist; divorce does not completely dissolve it. It changes the form of the relationship, but does not alter the relevance or the existence of the family. In the family approach to such situations, each family member is regarded as a participant in the decisions to be made, and the interests of no one person are deemed to override those of the others. The family approach endorses the preservation of intergenerational continuity insofar as possible, on the premise that all family relationships are mutual and important. A need to give and to receive love exists in the children, in their parents, and in their grandparents too.

REFERENCES

1. E. Benedek and R. Benedek, New Child Custody Laws: Making Them Do What They Say, *The American Journal of Orthopsychiatry* 42,5 (1972) 825-834.

2. Somers v. Somers, 146 N.W.2d 428 (Superior Court of Wis. 1966).

3. A. Demeter, LEGAL KIDNAPPING (Boston: Beacon Press, 1977) p 125.

4. See J. Birtchnell, Early Parent Death and Mental Illness, *British Journal of Psychiatry* 116,532 (1970) 281-288; _____, Depression in Relation to Early and Recent Parent Death, *British Journal of Psychiatry* 116,532 (1970) 299-306; and _____, The Relationship Between Attempted Suicide, Depression and Parent Death, *British Journal of Psychiatry* 116,532 (1970) 307-313.

5. Group for the Advancement of Psychiatry, THE JOYS AND SORROWS OF PARENTHOOD, GAP Report No. 84 (New York: GAP, 1973) pp 302-304.

6. No description of this phenomenon has been noted in the literature, but all of the members of the committee have observed examples in their practice.

7. Smith v. Smith, 15 Utah 2d 36 386 P.2d 900 (1963).

5

DIVORCE THERAPY OR COUNSELING

The official, legal process of a divorce can be described in a series of dated events—beginning with one of the partner's initial contact with a lawyer, culminating with the final divorce decree and ending with a decision relating to the custody of the children. The emotional process of a divorce cannot be so tidily described; its beginning may be elusive and entangled in events long past; its completion usually comes much later than the legal divorce—if it comes at all.

Divorce as an emotional process

A successfully completed divorce is one in which the two partners in a marriage are able to separate and subsequently relate to each other with a sense of comfort and an ability to recognize the individuality of each. The process of emotional disengagement following divorce takes time; it is difficult and often stormy. To a greater or lesser degree, it is associated with each partner's blindness to his or her own shortcomings in the relationship, a sense of having been victimized, a need to denigrate the other spouse, and a wish for retribution. Sometimes the hate, bitterness, and yearning for revenge conceal a latent wish for reparation and healing. More often, these negative feelings can be understood as a necessary emotional part of the divorce, a stage to be traversed on the way out of the marriage.[1]

893

It recalls the manner in which some students disparage their formerly admired and beloved school setting in order to be able to graduate and leave it. In some divorces, however, the spouses become stuck in this venomous phase for a long time.

For the emotional divorce process to be carried to its natural conclusion and resolution, it is essential that the death of the marriage be recognized, and the loss be mourned, which includes the relinquishing of the hopes and dreams that spawned and sustained the marriage. This painful process is expressed in an emerging understanding and acceptance of one's own role in contributing to the marital disharmony and the demise of that marriage.[2]

An introspective colleague, in a discussion of these issues, described with vivid clarity a moment which summed up for her the shift to a completed divorce. She had been visiting her adolescent son who lived with her ex-husband in another state. As she got into her car, preparing to drive back to her home, she turned and waved goodbye. And in that instant, she felt the anger and the bitterness were gone. Her ex-husband no longer looked terrifying to her; instead he appeared to be a rather nice looking man with some traits she did not care for. While driving home, she felt some sorrow about the pain they had inflicted on each other and regret for the wasted years—when they both knew they were drifting in a marriage that had failed. But, with all of the sadness, she felt free and able to move on with her life.

Many divorcing partners, in time, are able to reach a completed or "psychological divorce," but some seem unable to do so. The process of disengagement is sometimes so painful that one tries to avoid it, often at great psychological cost. In that sense, the reluctance to deal with the realities of divorce is not unlike that observed in coping with the realities of death. In both situations, there is difficulty in dealing with the sense of hopelessness, distress, and aimlessness generated by the end of a relationship.

In divorce, however, the legal process itself often delays the appropriate mourning. The adversary process, with two spouses in conflict—each championed by a lawyer—does not help the principals recognize and accept personal responsibility for the failure of the marriage.[3] A court battle hardens the lines drawn earlier in the couple's pre-divorce conflicts, and these lines may remain hardened indefinitely, especially if there is a child custody arrangement that is abrasive and unsatisfying to either ex-spouse.

During the legal phase of the divorce, each spouse typically professes love, concern, and a sense of responsibility for the children. The spouses vie to be seen as the preferred, more capable, more responsive parent. In this battle, which aims at victory for one spouse and defeat for the other, the children become victims. It is crucial to recognize that the parents are generally unaware of what is happening to them and to their children. The major task for all the professionals—both in law and in mental health—is to develop processes in which the divorcing parents can deal adequately with their negative feelings and disengage constructively.

Therapy or counseling for divorcing families

Divorce therapy or counseling is one viable mode of assistance. It seems to have grown out of a realization of the need to help people whose marriage has irrevocably broken down. As the divorce rate has escalated, there has been increasing emphasis upon counseling partners before, during, and after divorce in order: 1) to neutralize their continuing antagonism, so often associated with maladaptive responses in children; 2) to give each of them a better awareness of themselves as individual and separate persons; and 3) to identify and strengthen those com-

mon interests and goals around which members of the frag-
mented family may be able to rally.

Depending on the stage of the actual separation, the reasons
for coming to divorce counseling vary. Early in the process, the
reasons usually involve the reactions of one or both partners to
the impending breakup of the marriage. Many of the families
currently seeking divorce therapy are those in which the
partners have intense emotional relationships with each other
and in which there is an uneven motivation to dissolve the
marriage. One partner, more usually the woman, tends to feel
"dumped." Strategies for the counseling vary with individual
families, but the main thrust involves helping them face the
reality of divorce and the loss involved. Later, as the inevitabil-
ity of the divorce begins to be accepted, the reasons for seeking
help, more commonly, are linked to problems regarding the
child or children. The counselor's responsibility then includes
helping the parents to recognize the feelings the child is likely
to be experiencing.

It is currently important for each parent to become aware of
the enormous guilt that often resides in the first child of a
marriage, rooted in such observations as "We are staying together because of the child." Comments like these cannot help
but suggest to the child that his role is to be the glue between
unhappy parents. Later, when the divorce becomes a reality, he
cannot help but feel he has failed in his mission to keep the
parents together. If parents cannot keep themselves happy, a
child tends internally to assume the responsibility for their
unhappiness.

Part of the child's sense of guilt is actually rooted in reality,
since because of his very existence, his parents have been trans-
formed from husband and wife to father and mother. In this
transformation, previously hidden conflicts between the new
father and his own father often become reactivated and ex-

pressed in a variety of ways, thereby contaminating the marriage and the new family. Similarly for the new mother; her dormant struggle with her own mother may also erupt unexpectedly into view.

Many divorce therapists feel that, aside from the difficulties engendered by the adversary process, the main complication in divorce is the clients' perceptions of the reactions of their own parents.[4]

It is essential that each ex-spouse achieve an emotional separation from his or her family of origin in order for the divorce process to be satisfactorily completed. The issue for an ex-spouse in divorce is not so different from that during childhood, adolescence and young adulthood, namely, to achieve a more secure sense of self and to become more differentiated from one's family of origin.

Problems of divorce thus really involve three-generations. This suggests another approach that can be utilized in divorce counseling, that is, to include ex-spouses with their families of origin, as well as with their children. The focus of attention needs to be on the developmental phases of the life cycle, including the fantasies and events accompanying these phases.

Counseling with the entire family

The helplessness and confusion a person experiences during and immediately after divorce usually has a history that connects back to or reminds him of other changes in the life cycle, such as a sense of anxiety at leaving home to go to school for the first time. The divorce counselor's job is to have the parents and children articulate and share those negative experiences of earlier family life which have now become associated with the dissolution of the family. Another job of the divorce counselor is to make it clear that a divorce severs only the legal bond between the spouses. The legal and moral responsibility for the continued care of their children remains.

One problem in all counseling and therapy is the way the parties continue to interact in old patterns. This happens partly because they lack awareness of how they are perceived by others. For this reason, recordings on audio and video tape can be productively used in counseling sessions. The playback of segments of taped sessions with each spouse allows each of them to become observers of themselves and helps them see themselves as they are perceived by the rest of the family. Only by recognizing how they are seen by others can the spouses directly view themselves as free of their own self-justifying or self-righteous fantasies. Visible evidence that demonstrates facial expressions, vocal tones, and body language is very impressive; it can speed up the process and ease the way for the participant to become more responsible for himself or herself.

This kind of feedback can also work productively to prevent an emotional "cut-off," that is, a denial of meaningful connectedness between one's self and one's family of origin, one's spouse or ex-spouse, and one's children. Such cut-offs are generally related to an individual's difficulty in coping with psychic pain. Rather than have that pain resurrected or intensified, the individual distances himself from the person associated with the pain by becoming rigid and unresponsive. This can begin to be neutralized through dialogues and group meetings with the persons involved so that all participants experience accepting themselves as separate persons with their own joys and sorrows.

In divorce counseling, the task is to avert cut-offs between the ex-spouses and between the divorced parents and their children. It is important for the development of the child that he be able to express his feelings of guilt and also the hurt he has experienced from the divorce. It is important too that these experiences be shared with the parents as well as with the therapist so that the child can obtain relief from his painful feelings and fantasies by constructive feedback from the parents. The following case illustrates some of these points.

Case Example:
Counseling Prior to Legal Action

In September of 1973, Henry and Alice D, a successful journalist and his wife, both in their mid-thirties, consulted a family therapist about the impossibility of continuing their eight-year marriage. They had two children, a six-year-old girl, Wendy, and a four-and-one-half-year-old boy, Henry, Jr.

During that first consultation, parts of which were recorded on video tape for subsequent playback, the therapist learned that this was a first marriage for both and that they were in love when they got married. Their relationship had become strained during Alice's pregnancy with Wendy. Henry stated that he really had not been ready for a child at that time and that he had felt pushed, almost "blackmailed," into agreeing to the baby. Though the relationship between the two continued to be strained and tense, neither Alice nor Henry wanted Wendy to be an only child, and they hoped that another pregnancy might improve the situation. However, since Henry Jr.'s birth, Mr. D began to have repeated episodes of impotence, which increasingly alarmed him. His anxiety about it propelled him into at least four affairs.

Alice also had found their relationship more difficult and unpleasant since her pregnancy with Wendy. During the previous year, in late September 1972, Alice had unexpectedly found Henry in bed with Mary Beth, a 24-year-old married close friend of theirs. Alice had returned two days earlier than expected from a visit to her sister in New Hampshire. She had had the children with her for a projected seven-day visit, but had returned earlier because Wendy had fractured her elbow during a fall. Alice's reaction to finding Henry with Mary Beth was an uncontrollable rage, which was observed by the children. She demanded that Henry leave the house. He fought against this, professing love for his children from whom he did not wish to be separated so precipitously. Alice contended that he had rarely exhibited any fondness or affection for either child. Henry said that he had been concerned that Alice would harm the children, which he mentioned in front of their frightened children.

Henry did leave the house one month later, moving into an apartment with one of his female colleagues. In early December, after Alice became sexually involved with Mary Beth's husband, she decided to get a divorce. In January of 1973, Alice consulted an attorney to assist her in preparing for the divorce and in planning to take custody of the children. Alice's mother and sister supported this move to make "the break from Henry complete" for the sake of the children. Henry became enraged when served with divorce papers and refused to continue financial support for his family. Court litigation was initiated by Alice. Because of the escalating proportions of the acrimony, both attorneys recommended divorce counseling.

During that first session, the therapist also learned that Henry's mother had died from cancer of the breast, which had been discovered one year before his son's birth. As Henry reviewed his mother's illness and death, he became acutely aware that he had blamed Alice for years for the poor relationship that had existed between her and his mother. Alice protested, adding that she had never felt welcome at his parents' home, although she had attended to birthday cards and Christmas presents from Henry and the children to his parents.

Mutual recriminations were reactivated and escalated until a segment of their video-recorded reactions were played back to them. Almost immediately, Henry became visibly shaken to see how cold and distant he appeared. As his anger subsided, embarrassed shock took its place. Alice was surprised that Henry had been so unaware of his provocative and chilly manner. She, in turn, was distressed to see how much of a "bitch" there was in her. This painful self-confrontation on video tape coupled with the therapist's firm position that each had made a contribution to both the positive and the negative aspects of the marriage, enabled them both to agree to continue the divorce counseling process.

The first session concluded on the note that each spouse would be seen alone once and that the therapist would maintain confidentiality about what had been said to him in that session. The therapist indicated that his goal was to evolve a less angry and explosive relationship between the two spouses, so that co-parenting and decision making about the children could be more comfortably achieved. He asked each of them to communicate to him in writing any constructive thoughts they might have about visiting rights and other matters which might aid in the resolution of this "aggravated mess." He added that he would discuss with each party whatever the other had communicated in writing.

The therapist indicated that he wanted to see both of them together after the individual sessions. He also said that after the second joint visit he would like to see them both with the children to learn the extent of the children's distress about their parents' continuing turmoil. He instructed the parents to bring, for the session with the children, three pictures drawn free-hand—one of themselves at any point during their life, another of their family of origin, and a third of themselves in relation to the present family. Each child was instructed to draw three pictures as well, one of themselves, one with their family in an activity, and one with their family resting. These pictures were to be drawn alone, without being viewed by any other family member. At the conclusion of this exercise, the three drawings were to be placed in a sealed envelope, to be opened in the office settting.

During the individual session, Henry indicated that he had always been inclined to hold back on sharing his true feelings with anyone. He said that he had married Alice in the hope that she might somehow assist him to become more open and responsive, but this had never materialized. He dwelled for some time on his lingering shock that "that image" on the monitor was really himself. He thought he saw the punitive face of his father for a brief moment and wondered with disbelief how he could not have known this before since he observed himself shaving in the mirror each morning. He could see that such an expression would be difficult for a wife and children to cope with. He indicated reluctantly that he was pleased to have the opportunity to review some things that had troubled him for many years.

Alice's individual session revealed her chronically unsuccessful attempts to feel accepted by her mother, who seemed to be gifted, according to Alice, in locating all of her flaws. She remembered vividly, when she was in college, how she felt compelled to find someone to marry so that she would not have to go home for visits. She also indicated an interest in continuing the divorce counseling.

The therapist made it clear to each that he felt that an inability to acknowledge and accept one's complicity in the marital failure, however justified this might seem, renders one prone to re-creating similar patterns in subsequent relationships.

The second conjoint session with Alice and Henry was distinctly different from the first one; the anger level had subsided considerably and each was willing to review viable and reasonable visitation rights. The financial arrangements had been worked out concurrently by their attorneys and each had accepted with more resignation than anger that a divorce was the wiser course of action.

In the next session, the fifth in the series, the children came with their parents and their pictures. It was interesting to note that Henry, Jr., had, in the pictures of himself and his family, represented himself as a dot in the opposite corner from the family, whom he represented as stick figures. It became clear that he had been terrified by the recent events; he reported monster dreams and recounted with bitter tears the scene of the intense parental argument he had witnessed. It was quite apparent that Wendy, too, was very frightened as she described recent nightmares of "biting sharks." Assisted by the therapist, Alice and Henry were able to see the extent to which they had unwittingly frightened the children.

In the sixth session, with Alice and Henry alone, there was a review of how to cope with the children so that they could be less frightened by what was happening. The therapist was insistent that, whenever either Alice or Henry was going to be away, the children know in advance; also, the children should have phone numbers available where the parents could be reached.

Both Henry and Alice requested to see the therapist alone again. During this second set of individual sessions, each was concerned about the possible failure of a subsequent marriage. In an attempt to deal with this issue, the therapist suggested that each one should have a session with their families of origin. Henry was reluctant to bring in his father, but finally decided to do so. Alice came with her mother and sister. Her father had died during her freshman year in college. Henry's two siblings were living abroad and unavailable. After their respective family meetings, each felt more comfortable. This response opened up for each a further review of their relationships with their siblings and parents. Also evoked in each of them were hitherto unavailable memories of some early frightening sexual experiences.

In the eleventh session, Henry and Alice came without the children. They reviewed the video tape of the first session, which affirmed for them how much they had achieved in resolving the angry tensions beween themselves. In the twelfth and final session they came in with the children, who seemed to be more spontaneous and open. The parents spoke openly about having achieved a joint custody arrangement which would be part of the divorce agreement. Plans were made for a return visit with the children one year later.

The two subsequent annual visits with the children revealed the continued openness observed in the twelfth session. The children had grown both in size and in the richness of their new relationships in school.

Case Example:
Counseling After Divorce

The following case, which might be considered mild with regard to the duration and intensity of the problems that surfaced, did have the potentiality of escalating into chronic smoldering and periodic intensive quarreling, as during the last years of the marriage. It also had within it a number of typical post-divorce problems which, fortunately, were able to be resolved.

Mr. and Mrs. Y, who had been divorced less than a year, were in strong disagreement about whether to send their older child to the public school kindergarten or to enroll him in a private school with a religious affiliation. The question of counseling came up when the teachers at the nursery school noticed that the boy, who previously was socializing well, had started to withdraw and become fearful.

The parents originally met in New York City where they were both working. The father, aged 38, is the youngest of three brothers in a wealthy midwestern family. He did not want to join the family business and he became an attorney instead. Although he passed the bar, he never practiced law. His major interests are recording and radio broadcasting; he has had a few jobs in the field and has begun to be known in the industry. The mother, aged 32, is the oldest of three siblings in a modest French Canadian family. She came to New York after graduation from high school and was working as a secretary when she met her husband-to-be. Even though she recognized his tendency to be shy, she looked up to him because of his wealth, education and sophistication, including his command of the English language which she admires to this day.

Mr. Y was also very attracted to her, and after a few dates, they agreed to live together. After about two years, they decided to get married and move to California, where the husband felt he would have better career opportunities, and where the wife felt she could pursue her interests in painting.

They had two children, a four-year-old boy, Jean, and a three-year-old girl, Marie. Both parents agreed that things had gone downhill following the birth of the second child, when they began to have intense quarrels. Mrs. Y felt she had always been dominated by her husband, whom she saw as moody and easily angered, and she felt a need to be "free." Although Mr. Y felt unsupported by his wife in his entrepreneurial efforts—she wanted him to get a regular job—he, too, felt the quarrels made the situation intolerable.

An attempt at joint therapy seemed to demonstrate that the differences between them could not be bridged and they decided to split up. At that point, they had been married about eight years. Both agreed, however, that they did not want their separation to hurt the children unnecessarily; they promised that each would do everything possible to be maximally available to the children.

Following the example of a New York Times article on "co-parenting," they agreed that they would each have their own apartment, that the children would remain in the original home, and that they would alternate staying in the home and caring for the children. This arrangement failed, largely because the mother, who had also returned to work, felt she was not seeing enough of the children, even during "her" weeks of caring for them.

The mother then assumed primary custody and the father had liberal visiting privileges, taking the children to his apartment every other weekend and at least once during the week. There were definite tensions between them and occasional quarrels as they negotiated the formal divorce and custody agreements. They were able to "work things out," but tension still manifested itself from time to time over details about visiting.

As part of the divorce arrangements, Mrs. Y moved to a different nearby community with the children. Within a short time, a major disagreement between Mr. and Mrs. Y erupted over the question of whether to send Jean to kindergarten in a private school or in the public school. After both parents separately visited the public and private schools, Mr. Y wanted the public school because he felt it was good and also because of his own negative experiences in private schools. Mrs. Y leaned to the private school because she felt it would be better for Jean, who was somewhat shy, and because of its low-key religious affiliation. Mrs. Y became furious when Mr. Y in the midst of an argument about the subject, angrily said he would not pay for private school; she felt he was trying to dominate her again.

While all this was going on, Jean, a bright but somewhat shy four-year-old who had started to open up and socialize at nursery school, suddenly began to withdraw and regress. The teachers, who knew about the marital status of the parents, discussed the matter with their regular social work consultant who immediately called the mother in for a conference. At that time, the information about the school quarrel came out. The worker also felt that Jean was experiencing anxiety in relation to his father and suggested that the mother advise the father to do "something special" with Jean alone.

The father agreed, but the special excursion turned out to be a "fiasco." On the way home, Jean burst into tears and said he wanted to go to the "Mommy house" and not to the "Daddy house." Next weekend, Mrs. Y told Mr. Y that Jean had said that he did not want to stay with his father that weekend and also that he did not like the sound of his father's voice—it sounded "angry."

Mr. Y became very concerned that he might "lose" the boy and agreed to some joint meetings with the worker. There were four altogether. The first two, about one week apart, consisted largely of an outpouring of anger and resentment by both Mr. and Mrs. Y. The worker tried to clarify for them what they were angry about and also gave some information about the schools in question. Mr. Y later reported that he had never before realized how angry his wife was about remote as well as recent events. Mrs. Y recognized that Mr. Y was not trying to force her to do things his way but was genuinely concerned—for his own reasons—about what was best for Jean. She also became aware that Jean may have overheard telephone conversations in which she clearly showed her anger to his father.

Almost immediately after these first two interviews, Jean again seemed to open up in his behavior, at school and with his parents.

The next two interviews focused on the communication patterns between the parents and their assumptions about each other. Although both were pained by the fact of the divorce, neither wanted a resumption of the marriage; they were both relieved to know that the other felt similarly. Mrs. Y, especially, was relieved when she recognized that her ex-husband was not trying to manipulate her back into the marriage by using his money. Throughout, the worker acknowledged their mutual concern for the children and emphasized how important it was that they express their anger directly to each other about what may be bothering them at any given time.

Shortly thereafter, the mother took the children on a long summer vacation to her parents' home in Quebec. She reported that Mr. Y seemed much better after that vacation. She felt that the joint interviews "started something," but also that her ex-husband had changed for the better. "It is nice not quarreling," she observed.

Mr. Y, in turn, believed that because of the counseling both of them understood each other better and, as a result, both had changed. He further felt that there was something about the structure—they were divorced from each other and it was final—and also the timing that enabled them to accept what they could not before. Though divorced, they each were able to trust that the other would do his or her part as a parent. As an example, he cited the following situation that occurred recently.

Both children were visiting him, and Marie became angry over something. In her tears, she cried, "I hate you. I won't ever come and visit you again." This time, however, Mr. Y did not feel threatened, and asked her what she said when she was angry with her mother. Marie giggled, hid her eyes with her hand, and said, "The same thing." When Mr. Y described the incident to his ex-wife, she laughed and responded that when angry Marie sometimes says, "I hate you; I will go live with Daddy." And they both laughed—in joint recognition of their parental alliance.

Currently, Mr. Y is looking for a home near Mrs. Y's so that they can set up a joint custody arrangement. They both feel it can work now, and that it would offer advantages to both of them as well as the children. It would allow more flexibility in caring for the children, with less formality about visiting. It would allow more freedom for Mrs. Y as Mr. Y would take on more day-to-day caring for the children. It would also allow more freedom for Mr. Y to arrange for out-of-town trips in relation to his work, which is slowly moving ahead. Jean, incidentally, is in public school and continuing to do well.

Certainly, there are many aspects of this case that go beyond what has been summarized. But it does exemplify how a brief intervention at a critical time can alter the course of events. It also illustrates how easily children pick up and respond to parents' feelings and, how, in their day-to-day struggles to cope, children use whatever is going on, to express their own feelings. The parents, even if divorced from each other, must be helped to work together for the benefit of their children and not fall into the traps that children inadvertently set for them. Practically, this means getting some understanding about the children's behavior and, more important, learning how to separate their suspicions about each other from their concerns about the children.

Family workshops and camps

Recognizing the large numbers of children with problems stemming from the divorce of their parents, various courts and conciliation courts have developed workshops for families going through divorce, with special sessions for children.[5] These generally involve role-playing, both for the children and the adults, and opportunities for group discussions.

One such program, developed in Topeka, Kansas, by the Shawnee County Domestic Relations Court and the Community Service Office of the Menninger Foundation, made use of video tape presentations.[6] The workshop itself had four aims: 1) to help families understand the impact of divorce on their lives; 2) to help the divorcing parents understand the emotional needs of the children and deal with them; 3) to help the children deal with the emotional traumas of divorce; and 4) to help the parents develop the skills necessary to cope with the complications in living brought on by divorce (visitation, custody, support, etc.).

An important aspect of the program was a pair of video presentations, entitled "Breakup" and "Pain Games."[7] The first focused on the emotional shock that children of divorce experience and the second on the pain and anger felt by the parents but unknowingly and unintentionally passed on to the children as the parents tried to cope with their new situations.

In addition to the presentations, the program included various didactic presentations and opportunities for group discussion. The main goal was to help parents "realize they still have to communicate about the problems of parenting children, but they can no longer communicate with each other as husband and wife." This program, like other group programs, enabled the participants, especially the children, to gain relief by showing that others were going through the same situation, and that they were not alone in their concerns. The program had the full support of the judges who had participated in one of the workshops themselves.[8]

A different workshop experience is provided by the Family Life Center of Rochester, New York, a Catholic group which sponsors a one-week summer family camp for separated/ divorced parents and their children.[9] The camp sessions include recreation, rap sessions, and prayer sessions. These children, too, seem to get a lot out of interacting with other children in similar circumstances.

Conclusion

Independent of the specific technique used, the case examples illustrate the goal of a completed divorce. With regard to the divorcing partners, one works toward a diminution of feelings of failure and guilt and an increase in self esteem. This, in turn allows for a more balanced and accepting view of the ex-spouse. If strong differences remain, they are confronted directly and not fought out via the children; instead there is recognition of enough common interest in the children to allow for reasonable co-parenting. With regard to the children, there is a recognition of the pain and trauma they have been experiencing, and a commitment to diminish that as much as possible. Finally, regardless of who initiated the separation process, there is a recognition that the divorce is real and that both ex-spouses need to separate themselves emotionally from each other.

Divorce counseling, however limited in its capacity to solve contentious and bitter marital issues, offers a good possibility for diminishing the hatred in divorce that spills over and involves the children. Even if the anger itself is not resolved, there is evidence that, with help, it can often be deflected away from the children, so that a truce area or "demilitarized zone" can be constructed around them. Therefore, whenever children are involved, divorce counseling should be recommended by the courts, and the attorneys should be encouraged to refer families for such help.

Research is needed to discover more effective techniques for use in divorce counseling. Such research should consist of 1) an assessment of different kinds of intervention, such as individual or family therapy or group workshops; 2) the use of audio and video tape; and 3) the length, spacing, and number of sessions. Though a variety of research studies have disclosed a relationship between the age of the children at the time of divorce and the ways their development is impeded, more definitive long-range studies are necessary to determine in what ways children's growth may be protected or promoted by various techniques in divorce counseling.

REFERENCES

1. K. Kressel, M. Lopez-Morillas, J. Weinglass and M. Deutsch. "Professional Intervention in Divorce: The Views of Lawyers, Psychotherapists, and Clergy," in DIVORCE AND SEPARATION, George Levenger and Oliver Moles, eds (New York: Basic Books, 1979).

2. K. Kressel and M. Deutsch. Divorce Therapy: An In-Depth Survey of Therapists' Views, *Family Process* 16,4 (1977) 411-443.

3. Ibid., p 425.

4. Ibid., p 424.

5. P. Woolley, THE CUSTODY HANDBOOK (New York: Summit Books, 1979) p 668.

6. Video taped "pain games" help children in divorce situations. Roche Report: *Frontiers of Psychiatry* 9,3 (1979) 1-2.

7. "Pain Games" II: Developed and copyrighted by the Johnson County Mental Health Center, Olathe, Kansas.

8. See note 6, supra, p 2.

9. Family Camp for Separated/Divorced Parents and Their Children, *Marriage and Divorce Today* 5,52 (Aug. 4, 1980).

6

THE LITIGATION PROCESS AND THE MENTAL HEALTH PROFESSIONAL

In the previous chapters, we have described the trauma that a divorce causes, how the divorce often affects adversely the entire family, and how parents can be helped to pay proper attention to their children's needs through their own efforts, or, if that is impossible, through counseling of various types. Some divorcing couples, however, continue to fight over the custody of their children, literally, to the bitter end. In these instances, formal litigation is required which culminates in a court-imposed solution.

The goal of this chapter is to identify some of the special issues that arise in child custody disputes. It is not a manual of procedure,[1] but its goal is to provide a viewpoint and an orientation to the court system so that, with the help of the attorneys involved, the mental health professional can function constructively and effectively during the litigation process.

In this chapter, we will also examine the way the mental health professional enters a given case, performs the examination, and makes the recommendations. In addition, we will also discuss some aspects of the court's fact finding and decision making function. Finally, we will present some ways of by-passing adversary system battles, including the use of joint custody.

Court process

Although it is increasingly recognized that the adversary system is not really suited to the resolution of family differences, it

913

remains as the structure within which intractable disputes have
to be resolved. Its major defect, of course, is that it accentuates
differences rather than diminishes them. One of its most elo-
quent critics is Judge Byron F. Lindsley who said:

> The adversary process, historically effective in resolv-
> ing disputes between litigants where evidentiary facts
> have probative significance, is not properly suited to
> the resolution of most family relations problems. . .
> Where there are children and the parties cannot or will
> not recognize the impact of the disintegration of the
> marriage upon the children, where they fail to perceive
> their primary responsibilities as parents—i.e., custody
> and visitation—we make it possible for parents to carry
> out that struggle by the old, adversary, fault-finding,
> condemnation approach . . . This kind of battle is de-
> structive to the welfare, best interests, and emotional
> health of their children.[2]

Although traditional adversary procedures are used in child
custody litigation in most jurisdictions, an increasing number
of jurists are seeking ways to avoid or minimize the harmful
effects of such practices. Some courts have done more than
others in this regard. But it should be recognized that, since
each state is responsible for its own laws and its own courts, the
legal arrangements for deciding disputed child custody cases
vary considerably.

In some jurisdictions, the judges handling divorce and child
custody cases rotate at frequent intervals, and the implied attitude is that these cases are not much different from contract
disputes or criminal prosecutions. In most jurisdictions, however, the rotation is infrequent; one or more judges handle
domestic cases and they serve long enough so that they develop
some expertise in dealing with such cases. In some few jurisdictions, however, there are specific family or domestic relations

courts which attempt to deal with the special needs of the litigants.

The courts in almost all jurisdictions have some independent investigative or fact finding capacity; this is most often exercised through the county probation department. In disputed cases, these court workers will interview relatives, friends and the principals, and develop recommendations for the court regarding the pending litigation. In some jurisdictions, there are also conciliation courts which have the additional goal of helping the divorcing parents try to come to agreement about custody and visitation arrangements. In a few jurisdictions, the courts have a panel of mental health professionals available; sometimes one of them may be called in as a "friend of the court" when special problems exist which cannot be fully dealt with by the existing court agencies.

Conciliation courts

As the term conciliation court suggests, it was originally set up to explore the possibility of reconciliation in parties filing for divorce. First established in Los Angeles in 1939, it gradually expanded its services to include divorce counseling. It served as a model, both for the State of California and the rest of the country, and today there are about 150 such courts throughout the country, mostly in urban areas.[3]

Conciliation courts are designed to give immediate help and guidance to families approaching the court for divorce. If the family seems interested in reconciliation, it will be helped in that direction. If the family, however, is committed to divorce, as are the majority of families who have come this far, the staff tries to help the families adjust to the breakup of the marriage and to negotiate solutions to the custody and visitation issues.

These services are considered crisis-oriented rather than on-going counseling and there is usually a limit of six visits per family.[4] Some conciliation courts spend from twelve to fifteen hours with a family.[5] In some instances, the counseling is kept separate from the custody investigations, and is considered confidential. In other instances, a counselor may make a confidential report to the judge.[6] In still other instances, the counselors do the actual custody evaluations and report to the court.

The referrals to the conciliation courts are generally made prior to any court hearing, and in a large majority of the cases an agreement is worked out. Woolley[7] cites a study reporting that 90 percent of cases come to agreement with the help of the conciliation court.

Contribution of the mental health professional

The potential contribution of the mental health professional needs to be seen in the light of the goal of "transforming . . . [the] . . . battlefield into a peace conference" in concert with judges and attorneys who share the same objective.[8] It is our belief and that of other observers[9] that the inability to come to an agreement about the children's custody, with the consequent need for formal litigation in an adversary setting, represents a failure in the process of completing a psychological divorce. Why the process may have failed, at least up to that point, may be due to many factors. For example, the acute pain of the break-up may still be too great for the parties to think constructively about their children; or they may be too immature, or selfish to think beyond themselves; or they may be encouraged to fight by relatives and even their attorneys. Whatever the reason for failure, the willingness of the professionals to see the fact of litigation as a sign of failure in the human process may be the first step toward making the court process constructive—if the professionals can keep pushing the litigants toward negotiation and compromise. For some litigants, the power and the authority of the court can become the balancing positive factor that nudges them toward more reasonable positions.

Still it must be recognized that, in spite of all effort, some divorcing couples cannot or will not give up fighting through their children. In those instances, the mental health professional must be able to describe to the court what is happening and make recommendations on which the court can base its decisions. Therefore the mental health professional involved in the litigation process really has two tasks. The first is to explore the possibilities for negotiation and compromise between the parents. The second is to examine the family adequately and give the court enough information so that it can make an appropriate decision, but to do so in a way consistent with seeking peace between the warring factions.

Involvement of the mental health professional

The most common manner in which the mental health professional becomes involved in a child custody dispute is by a call from the attorney representing one of the parties. In the large majority of cases, it is from the attorney representing the husband or the wife, but in those few cases where the child is represented by an attorney, that attorney may make the original or first call.

The attorney calling describes the situation and asks that the client be interviewed and/or the child be examined with a view to determining the clinician's opinion about the child custody issue. The mental health professional is also informed about the factual situation and is advised that the criterion to be used is that of "the best interests of the child." The attorney will want a report after the examination, and the mental health professional will usually be expected to testify, assuming his or her opinion supports the position of the attorney's client.

At this point, two issues arise. The first is whether the mental health professional wants to become involved in the legal process at all. Even with the growth of courses and training programs in law and mental health, many mental health professionals prefer staying out of the legal arena. The decision is an individual one. But if the mental health professional decides to become involved, it is important that he or she understands the issues and has a clear concept of role.

The second question is that of defining the role. Will the mental health professional let himself be used in the traditional manner? Or will he or she press for an "expanded" role? This issue is critical and potentially influences the entire outcome. In the traditional role, the mental health professional is called by the attorney representing one of the parties. He/she does an examination of the child and of the party involved and, if the opinion agrees with that which the attorney wishes, testifies on a limited basis. The attorney then uses that testimony as a building block in his or her case.

The traditional involvement, therefore, has the mental health professional working with one side of the case. This involves the risk of an incomplete evaluation as well as that of overidentifying with that one side. Also, since situations are rarely black and white, the structure of working with one side sometimes makes it difficult to give an opinion showing all the nuances of the situation. Finally, there is the question of how the mental health professional is viewed by the court and other observers of the legal scene. To the extent that any health professional is seen as an "advocate who simply mimics or gives lip service" to the attorney's theory of the case, that professional is seen as "... reduced ... professionally to the level of a 'hired gun'."[10] Furthermore, such opinions are increasingly discounted by the more experienced courts.[11]

Importance of examining the entire family

Throughout this report, we have emphasized the importance of understanding the total family interaction. This position raises serious doubts about an unquestioning acceptance of just seeing one part of the family. It is extremely difficult, if not impossible, to adequately compare two sides of a family without looking at them equally. If one does not look at them equally, there is the risk of reaching conclusions based on examinational data about one side and assumptions about the other side, which in turn may be based on biased data.

It is sometimes possible, if called by one side, to ask to see the other side in order to make an adequate evaluation, and these requests are often agreed to. Seeing both sides, of course, creates a much better clinical situation. Even so, it is sometimes difficult to convince the court, and more important, the divorcing parents of one's objectivity. Therefore, it becomes extremely important to structure the involvement in the case so that the participants can feel the objectivity of the examiner. This is especially important because, valuable and necessary as the evaluation may be, its goal goes beyond the simple gathering of data. Its primary aim, we believe, is to explore the possibility of agreement between the parties in order to circumvent the destructive court battle. Failing that, it is important to develop the recommendations in an atmosphere that the court can use to encourage agreement.

Some mental health professionals do not feel strongly about seeing all members of the family, and are occasionally willing to function in a more limited fashion. But more and more

mental health professionals tend to agree about the broader
role and refuse to take on child custody cases unless there is
agreement in advance by both sides that all the relevant participants can be seen.

Developing policies about family evaluation

How to accomplish the goal of seeing the entire family depends
in part on the situation. If the mental health professional who
is called works for or is a member of a clinic, or an organized
group, the clinic or the group can have an agreed upon policy
with a prepared letter describing and explaining that policy so
that the information and the explanation can be given immediately on the phone and followed up by a letter. Similarly, if
the mental health professional who is called is in individual
practice, the position can be thought out in advance and the
explanation given at the time of the first call.

The general position might be that the individual or the
clinic would accept the case if some conditions were met. Some
typical conditions are: 1) that there is an agreement between the
attorneys that all the parties will be seen as indicated; 2) that a
report will go to both sides; and 3) that after an estimate of the
cost, there will be a commitment that the fees will be paid.

As clinics and individual practitioners develop policies for
participating in disputed child custody cases, the courts inevitably will develop a formal or informal list of those mental
health professionals who participate on the basis of doing a
complete examination of the family, thus creating for themselves a panel of family experts. Out of this panel, individual
attorneys would be able to choose experts in specific cases and
would know in advance what the policies and procedures
would be.

Until that time, however, arrangements to see the entire family have to be worked out on a case by case basis. In order to get agreement on these arrangements, it is sometimes helpful to meet with both attorneys to explain the procedure and the reasons for it. It is frequently helpful to meet with the divorcing parents to give them a similar explanation and to allay their doubts and fears. In dealing with the parents at the preliminary stage, it may be necessary to see each parent separately, particularly if they are so angry that they won't meet with each other.

Team evaluations

One advantage of involving a clinic or group of mental health professionals is that a team can take on the evaluation. Different mental health professionals can then deal with different members in the dispute. The process becomes similar to conjoint marital therapy, where the partners meet together with the counseling couple, and also individually with one of the counselors, who can be seen as identifying with that partner's individual postion. Furthermore, in a team evaluation, there is the possibility of the child being seen separately, and having his or her own adult ally, or advocate. The team would meet together for an exchange of information and the development of joint recommendations, but would focus on the process of facilitating agreement between the fighting husband and wife.

Content of evaluation

Whether the case is being evaluated by an individual or by a team, the goal should be the same—an evaluation of the interaction of the entire family, with particular attention to the quality of the parent-child interactions and of the capacity of the parents to deal with each other for the benefit of the children, both immediately and in the long term. To this end, each parent is seen individually, and each child is seen individually and together. Each parent is then seen with the children, and the parents are seen together without the children. Sometimes, if the emotional circumstances allow, the entire family is seen together.

Trunnell, a child psychiatrist, has described an outline for examination in child custody cases as follows:[12]

Questions to be answered:

Examination of child

1. Basic mental health status?
2. Previous development course?
3. Methods of coping, with particular attention to restoring missing parent and coping with grief?
4. Degree of attachment to parents?
5. Phase of development with particular attention to type of parenting indicated from both mother and father?
6. Degree and severity of any psychological impairment and treatment indicated, if any?
7. Ability to use substitute objects as resource in lieu of missing parent?

Examination of parents individually

1. Basic mental health status?
2. Personality functioning vis-a-vis ability to parent. Are there liabilities secondary to:
   a. neurotic unconscious concerns about dependency, power, anger, sexuality, defending against unhappiness using the child?
   b. specifically malignant psychopathological states (e.g., the Johnson-Szurek phenomena in fostering delinquency)?

      c. major pathology (psychosis, toxic substances abuse, character pathology)?
3. Past personal history with particular reference to their own childhoods?
4. Degree of flexibility in accepting feedback to their parenting responsibilities?
5. Probable method of restoring missing mate—cooperative or non-cooperative?
6. Ability to form treatment alliance where their children are concerned?

Examination of parents conjointly

1. How do personalities mesh in terms of filling out deficits for providing appropriate parenting as a dyadic unit?
2. How do personalities mesh in terms of being able to be minimally cooperative with their children?
3. How will future events affect them (e.g., remarriage of spouse)?

Examination of parent-child interaction

1. What is spontaneous response of child to parent—is parent viewed as asset—and if not, how come?
2. How in tune with the child is the parent—is the parent "listening" or "telling"?
3. How psychologically nurturing is the parent?

As these data are being gathered, the mental health professional is evaluating how to bring the angry, fighting forces together on behalf of the child or children. Trunnell, speaking from the perspective of child psychiatry, describes what we believe is a sound family approach, as follows:

    The task of building an alliance for the aid of the child is a complex one. There can be no established procedures, only principles. The first of these is attempting to build cohesiveness in the family, and sometimes this can be done by approaching the healthiest member and, through him or her, approaching the most disparate member. Surprisingly, often the healthiest and most accessible member is an articulate grade school child who, with the aid of a child psychiatrist, can tell it like it is. Often, the child's description of how bad he or she feels, when presented to both parents, may dislodge those parents from the adversary positions they have assumed around the child. Sometimes a healthier parent or step-parent or a relative may become the prime mover in the procedure of trying to obtain cohesion. Sometimes a conscientious attorney can persuade his client to heed medical advice for the benefit of the children involved. Sometimes we have an enlightened judge who can or will do this.[13]

On the basis of these interviews, and the process undertaken in them, the parents may be able to come to some agreement. If not, the findings are summarized and evaluated, and a report is prepared for the court, using the principles described in Chapter 4.

The next step, the presentation of the conclusions, is very important, if one bears in mind the goal—seeking agreement on custody whenever possible. Sometimes, the findings can be reported jointly to both sides in the continued hope of trying to reach some agreement. Most of the time, however, the findings must also be presented in a written report which goes to both sides and the court. Occasionally, on the basis of the written report, and the evaluation of its impact by the attorneys, a process leading to compromise and agreement can then be developed. Often, however, the findings have to be presented in a formal court hearing. (Information about the actual court testimony can be found in standard texts on psychiatry and the law and will not be presented here.)[14,15]

Reopened custody decisions

The above procedure has been described for cases in which the dispute about child custody is part of the original divorce action. In some instances, however, cases are re-opened after a particular custody decision has been in force for a greater or lesser period of time. The legal basis for re-opening such cases is an allegation of a significant change in the child's situation, or in the circumstances of the custodial or non-custodial parent. Sometimes, there is an allegation that the child has been neglected or abused, or has developed an emotional difficulty; often there is an accompanying allegation that the custodial parent is or has become unfit.

Generally, it is possible to evaluate the quality of the custodial home, how the custodial parent and child are getting along with each other, and whether there is something detrimental going on, as the non-custodial spouse often alleges. Depending on the specific allegations about the existing custody arrangement, it may be possible then to defend against them after an examination of the accused parent and the child. Since it is frequently possible to do an adequate examination with regard to the specific issues raised, some mental health professionals do accept such "defense" cases. Then, if the findings warrant it, they testify in favor of the status quo and against disturbing the existing arrangements.

This role of the mental health professional works satisfactorily if the allegations are not valid. Problems develop, however, if the examiner concludes after examination that the allegations are valid. Under those circumstances, the mental health professional might refuse to testify and might also try to get the attorney and client to work out a better arrangement for the child.

Looking beyond the specific allegations in a re-opened custody case, it should be clear that a re-opened case represents an unstable arrangement, an unsatisfactory previous solution. The nature of the instability may not be immediately apparent, but access to all of the principals opens the possibility of identifying the real hurts and exploring, perhaps for the first time, the possibility of finding a more stable custody arrangement. For that reason, many mental health professionals handle re-opened cases the same way as first time evaluations—by expecting to evaluate the total family system.

A study of the court process

As described earlier, most courts handling custody cases have personnel which can investigate facts and make recommendations regarding custody. When independent mental health professionals are called in to a custody case, it is usually to challenge or support the report by court staff. It is important, therefore, to know how such personnel function, and the following study throws some light on the matter.

McDermott et al.,[16] studied the process by which recommendations were made in a typical family court. The research group also developed, on an experimental basis, a Parent-Child Interaction Test (PCIT), a video taped sequence of parent-child behavior. In evaluating the actual criteria used by court workers, the researchers found that:

> Court workers were most concerned with satisfying the immediate physical and emotional needs of each child and did not address the longitudinal developmental issues that frequently concern clinicians. . . Because interactional and emotional criteria are less tangible and are more difficult to evaluate conclusively, practical criteria probably have been overemphasized in custody decisions.[17]

In general, the recommendations of the worker depended on the following criteria, in this order: 1) the level of physical care available; 2) the parent's past involvement with the care of the child, and apparent ability to provide support and understanding; 3) the "child's wishes"—validated by a superficial examination of the child's relationships with family members including siblings, and 4) a general assessment of the child's functioning. The data on which these judgments were based were, except for "physical care," difficult to obtain and of uncertain validity.

The authors found that the PCIT could be used as a sort of laboratory test to supplement the judgments of caseworkers.

> The parents' attachment behavior toward each child was analyzed according to such factors as empathy with and sensitivity to the child's own level, e.g., ability to sense and manage the child's needs, facility with discipline, guidance and consistency, patience, intellectual stimulation, facilitation of emotional expression, and spontaneity, physical closeness, encouragement, and acceptance.[18]

Court workers, who were invited to view the PCIT and incorporate the findings into their own evaluations, found the video tapes quite valuable. Their greatest value was in providing data on the emotional and psychological aspects of parent-child interactions in a manner that could be studied over and over until they became clear.

They also described some follow-up study for an unspecified number of cases:

> Comparisons between original PCIT's and those obtained one to two years later dramatically illustrated the effects of particular custody arrangements and criteria on child development and court-created family subsystems. Our results indicate that serious consideration should be given to termination of visitation rights in

cases in which a custodial parent adamantly opposes
visitation or strongly dislikes his other former spouse
and pressures the children to adopt similar attitudes. In
this regard, our study has supported the position taken
by Goldstein et al. Although the positive values of
maintaining regular contact with two parents are considerable, the stressful effects of necessarily balancing or
hiding attachment feelings for each parent appear to
have serious consequences for children as seen in
follow-up tapes one year later.[19]

In correspondence with us, McDermott et al., have emphasized that the number of cases in their sample where this was true
was extremely small.[20] They agree with our position that clinical judgment, not the feeling of the custodial parent, should be
the basis for making decisions about visitation, and they feel
that their method of checking clinical judgment is a means of
identifying such infrequent cases. While we acknowledge that
there may be some cases where visitation may have to be limited, it is important in such cases that the short term benefit
be weighed against the long term harm. (See Chapter 3.) We
believe that this is a difficult judgment; it should be carefully
weighed by skilled and balanced observers and not left to the
discretion of the custodial parent alone.

While one cannot generalize about court personnel from the
study of one court, the study does raise the question of the
working familiarity of court workers with mental health concepts. It also suggests an additional important role for the
mental health field—the education of court workers.

Clinical alternatives to litigation

For a long time, however, psychiatrists have been concerned
that disputed custody arrangements, and the visitation problems that so often follow such disputes, cannot really be

handled by the adversary system. In 1964, Kubie proposed an arrangement which he felt would protect the interests of children of divorced parents.[21] "The essence of the proposal consists of joint custody of the child, the appointment of a confidential adult ally for the child, and a committee chosen by the parents to decide questions on which the parents are unable to agree."[22]

Kubie reported that he has seen such committees function quite well, but more important, he points out that: "In practice, such committees have done more than solve disputes. Their mere existence often protects the parents from reaching an impasse. As a result, such committees have to be called into action only rarely."[23]

One outgrowth of the Kubie proposal is a plan developed by Solow and Adams.[24] Stressing psychiatric considerations above legal ones, they accept cases for custody evaluation only if both sides agree to be examined and also agree, by contract, to accept the psychiatric recommendations as binding. Clients also have to agree that they will meet with the psychiatrists six months later for follow-up evaluation. Neither parent waives the right to reopen the matter with the court, but the authors feel there has been no misuse of this right. They state:

> We have found that aiding parents to understand and to cooperate with the terms of the agreement has indeed reduced some of the painful sequels, and some of the continuing strife, which often attend custody litigation. . . . The involved household and their individual members have discovered that being required to deal in the arena of psychiatry, rather than the law, gives them a recourse preferable to the adversary system in which they previously have been embroiled. In this manner, the agreement has promoted continuity of intrafamilial relationships for the children, thus forestalling impulsive and stressful requests for change in the custody decree.[25]

Joint custody—A possible solution

The original Kubie proposal and the later Solow-Adams plan emphasize the joint sharing of parental responsibilities and the resolution of disagreements in a non-legal arena. The recent interest in joint custody (See Chapter 2) represents a wish on the part of divorcing parents to minimize the hurts and traumas of the divorce both for themselves and their children.

The term "joint custody," however, means different things to different people. It has also been labeled "shared custody," "divided custody," and "alternating custody."[26] The common element in all of these terms is that the child lives with each parent a substantial amount of time, allowing for a more realistic, normal relationship with each parent. In this arrangement, each parent assumes equal responsibility for the physical and psychological development of the child, and they share with each other equal responsibility for major decisions that affect the child.[27]

Attitudes to such an arrangement vary widely.[28] Some are strongly in favor, and others are equally opposed to it. A number favor it as a presumption; it would be used unless one of the parents shows that it would be "inappropriate."

The advantage of joint custody, if a satisfactory arrangement can be worked out, is that it is most likely to preserve for the child a meaningful access to both parents. Moreover, neither of the parents "loses" the child or becomes a visitor in the child's life.

The disadvantage of joint custody, even assuming that the parents are able to keep the child out of any residual battles between themselves, is that the child may continue to feel a sense of uncertainty and anxiety as he or she moves back and forth between two homes.

Some small studies have confirmed the advantages for the child, at least over a short term.[29,30] In San Francisco, an ongoing study of joint custody is nearing completion of its first phase.[31] In this study, divorced parents sharing custody of their children were sought out, and it therefore represents a group of cases, twenty-four in number, who volunteered or agreed to be studied. A look at the common characteristics of these "families" may be helpful.

Most of the parents in the study were middle class and well-educated; many were professionals. There was a wide income range, however, in the group. The work and family patterns were such that the mothers worked and the fathers generally shared in child caring before the divorce; the shift for many of them after divorce was not great. Most of the divorced parents continued to live in the same neighborhoods as their ex-spouses so that the childen had the same friends and attended the same schools, regardless of which home they were in at any given time. Where one spouse lived at a distance, he or she arranged for transportation of the child, often spending much time as a chauffeur.

It was noted that a large number of the parents had had counseling or psychotherapy prior to, or while in the process of, setting up the joint arrangement. Also, these parents, while interested in their children, had the capacity to draw boundaries and not intrude into the lives of their ex-spouses. Finally, and most important, each parent expended a great deal of time and effort to make the plan work.

One observation about the children is significant. It appears that what was important for them was the access to both parents. The actual amount of time spent at each home did not have to be equal or balanced for them to feel positive about the plan.[32]

One important consideration: the mental health professional, to whom parents interested in joint custody might go for therapy or counseling, needs to understand the concept and be willing to work with the divorcing parents to achieve their goal. In the case of the Y family, described earlier, there was an abortive attempt at counseling the first time they tried to work out a joint custody arrangement. They quit in disgust when the therapist, in response to their expressed interest in a joint custody arrangement, kept interpreting that what they really wanted was a reconciliation.

In response to the question, "Is joint custody the solution?", the answer has to be, "Not for every family." The answer depends on the wishes, the motivations, and the capacities of the parents, and as the children get older, theirs as well.[33] Specifically, the parents need to be moving to an emotionally completed divorce. They need to have a strong commitment to resolve their disagreements outside of court and/or have a back-up counseling arrangement to help them do so.

While there are certain psychological advantages to the parents in a joint custody arrangement—neither "wins" or "loses" the children—the same kind of arrangement can often be worked out informally in a sole custody situation, if the parents can, in fact, agree about the care of their children. The critical factor is the capacity of the parents to come to agreement about the care of their children.

As we see it, the concept of joint custody is not a solution for parents unable to come to agreement. It definitely should not be imposed on a fighting couple as a way of compromising or resolving the dispute. Experience has shown that such an arrangement simply cannot work. Joint custody, we believe, should be a goal, an end for divorcing parents to work towards, assuming that both of them can see its value.

Conclusion

Based on the principle that a negotiated solution is preferable to a court-imposed verdict, the role of the mental health professional is to evaluate the family system and to explore what may be required for the divorcing parents to come to agreement about the care of their children. In order to be objective and to be seen as such, he has to examine the entire family, rather than evaluate the situation from the perspective of one side or the other.

Throughout the entire process, the mental health professional should actively explore the possibility for agreement, and if the clinical situation allows it, help the parties come to agreement. If agreement cannot be reached and the case does come to a formal hearing, the recommendations of the mental health professional should, as much as possible, encourage a diminution of fighting between the parents.

In this chapter, and in Chapter 5, we have also shown that there are a significant number of families who have been able to avoid litigation; many have used both court-related and private mental health facilities to resolve their difficulties, and some of these have established "joint custody" arrangements. Based on the evidence, we believe that some form of co-parenting after divorce, however labeled, is a viable arrangement, if both parties have the emotional capacity and the psychological commitment to resolve their differences by negotiation. Joint custody, however, is not a compromise solution to be imposed on parents actively fighting with each other. For it to work, both parents must want it and be ready for it. It does, however, remain as a goal for a divorced couple to work towards.

REFERENCES

1. See M. G. Goldzband, CUSTODY CASES AND EXPERT WITNESSES (New York: Harcourt Brace Jovanovich, 1980).

2. B. F. Lindsley, Custody Proceedings: Battlefield or Peace Conference, *Bulletin of the American Academy of Psychiatry and the Law* 4,2 (1976) 127-131.

3. P. Woolley, THE CUSTODY HANDBOOK (New York: Summit Books, 1979) p 331.

4. Ibid., p 268.

5. Tucson Conciliation Court Establishes Child Custody/Visitation Service, *Marriage and Divorce Today* 6,1 (Aug. 11, 1980) p 2.

6. Ibid.

7. See note 3, p 331.

8. See note 2, p 127.

9. K. Kressel and M. Deutsch, Divorce Therapy: An In-Depth Survey of Therapists' Views, *Family Process*, 16,4 (1977) p 422.

10. S. S. Franklin, M. T. Hunt, T. Vogt et al., Hypertension and Cerebral Hemorrhage: A Malpractice Controversy, *Western Journal of Medicine* 133,2 (1980) 139.

11. Judge Michael Ballachey, Personal Communication, June 18, 1980.

12. T. L. Trunnell, Johnnie and Suzie, Don't Cry: Mommy and Daddy Aren't That Way, *Bulletin of the American Academy of Psychiatry and the Law* 4,2 (1976) 120-126.

13. Ibid., p 124.

14. Ralph Slovenko, PSYCHIATRY AND LAW (Boston: Little, Brown & Co., 1974).

15. See note 1.

16. J. F. McDermott, W. S. Tseng, W. F. Char, and C. S. Fukunaga, Child Custody Decision Making, the Search for Improvement, *Journal of the American Academy of Child Psychiatry* 17,1 (1978) 104-116.

17. Ibid., p 110

18. Ibid., p 112.

19. Ibid., p 114.

20. J. F. McDermott, Personal Communication, Sept. 28, 1978.

21. L. S. Kubie, Provisions for The Care of Children of Divorced Parents: A New Legal Instrument, *Yale Law Journal* 73 (1964) 1197-1200.

22. Ibid., p 1198.

23. Ibid., p 1200.

24. R. A. Solow and P. L. Adams, Custody by Agreement: Child Psychiatrist as Child Advocate, *Journal of Psychiatry and Law* 5 (1977) 77-100.

25. Ibid., p 90.

26. M. J. T. Cox and L. Cease, Joint Custody, *Family Advocate* (Summer 1978) pp 10-13, 42-44.

27. P. Woolley, Shared Custody, *Family Advocate* (Summer 1978) pp 6-9, 33-34.

28. E. P. Benedek and R. S. Benedek, Joint Custody: Solution or Illusion, *American Journal of Psychiatry* 136,12 (1979) 1540-1544.

29. A. Abarbanel, Shared Parenting After Separation and Divorce: A Study of Joint Custody, *American Journal of Orthopsychiatry* 49,2 (1979) 320-329.

30. J. B. Grief, Fathers, Children, and Joint Custody, *American Journal of Orthopsychiatry* 49,2 (1979) 311-319.

31. S. Steinman, THE EXPERIENCE OF CHILDREN IN A JOINT CUSTODY ARRANGEMENT: A REPORT OF A STUDY, [forthcoming].

32. Ibid.

33. See note 28, p 1543.

7

RECOMMENDATIONS TO THE COURTS

In our concern for the child's welfare throughout the phases of parental strife and divorce, we have emphasized the preservation of his organic community, his relationship to his family of origin. The child's need for "having" parents is absolute; it does not depend on the parents' psychological or socio-economic circumstances. Even "bad" relationships are often preferable to the prospect of unrelatedness.

We recognize that the courts can guide and enforce human arrangements only to a limited degree, since the law can neither create nor terminate the live process of human relationships. Even where social custom may fully endorse a court's position, the decision itself may represent only an official "cele-bration"—a ratification of clients' agreements—rather than any actual regulation of close human relationships.

Nevertheless, we believe that the court represents the general community interest that parties act responsibly. It should be willing to develop and use its power to that end, both in its own courtroom and in recommending necessary changes to legislatures.

Our recommendations fall into three areas: 1) procedures, 2) the decision-making process, and 3) post-divorce litigation.

With regard to procedures, the most obvious concern is about the harmful effects of traditional adversary processes. Even without extensive legal reform, much can be done by individual judges to reduce the harmful aspects of legal confrontation. Some suggestions include:

- reducing some of the non-essential formalities of the hearings;

- increasing the use of conferences in chambers with attorneys;

- conveying to all involved parties the value and the importance of their coming to agreement—at any stage of the litigation;

- where divorcing families seem to need more help than court attached workers can provide, courts should make referrals to divorce counseling as early as possible in the process; and, finally,

- courts should be aware that a divorce is a major crisis in the children's lives and that, therefore, the sooner the issues are resolved, the better.

With regard to the decision-making process, we recognize the court's final responsibility, but we do have some suggestions to offer. First, we think it is important that the court develop enough expertise in the area of mental health so that it can distinguish between a satisfactory evaluation and an unsatisfactory one. We believe that such a capacity can allow for more effective use of mental health professionals in these difficult cases.

We also have recommendations about the criteria used in decision making and respectfully offer them as follows:

- The court's determination should aim at providing the child with an ongoing relationship with as many members of his or her family of origin as possible. We are convinced that this is more helpful in the long run and less disruptive than a primary relationship with one parent and treating the non-custodial parent as though he or she were a visitor in the child's life.

- The court should not confirm the moral condemnation of one parent by the other since the child's welfare is badly served by the loss of trust such condemnations engender. In the adversary process of a court contest between the parents, phrased as a struggle on behalf of the child's best interests, the child may become the silent, helpless victim. It is to the child's advantage that all trust diminishing processes be minimized. A loss of trust in either parent is more damaging in the long run than most kinds of inadequate parenting behaviors.[1]

- In determining parental competence, the court should seriously consider the comparative willingness of the two contestants to provide the child with access to the other parent, to siblings, grandparents, and other relatives.

- The child should not be considered merely a passive recipient of parental care but also a concerned and willing soure of support for both parents. Regardless of the legal determinations of divorce and custody, the child has a need to express and channel concern about all family members, including the non-custodial parent.

As all of us know, the problems do not end with the court decisions on custody and related matters. Our suggestions to the court for this stage are based on the observation that continued post-divorce quarreling and litigation are signs that something is wrong in the equilibrium and that this now divorced "family" needs continued help. Whenever such difficulties become apparent, the court should encourage post-divorce counseling for the sundered family so as to diminish the quarreling and fortify common goals related to the development of the children.

Furthermore, the goal of minimal judicial interference should not be permitted to erode the court's role into one of silent collusion with irresponsible choices made for adult convenience. The court should be ready and able to "interfere" in re-evaluating custody determinations that are no longer satisfactory for the children.

Ultimately, of course, courts cannot force parents to become genuinely responsible. But we believe that the courts—by being knowledgeable about the mental health field, making appropriate referrals, and monitoring the outcome—can help create a process that will encourage the growth of responsibility in parents and thereby protect the interests of future generations.

REFERENCE

1. Ivan Boszormenyi-Nagy, "Contextual Therapy," Chapter in THE AMERICAN FAMILY [In press].

APPENDIX

A Uniform Marriage and Divorce Act (1970) Part IV—Custody

B Uniform Child Custody Jurisdiction Act

C Michigan Child Custody Act

D The Bill of Rights of Children in Divorce Actions

A

UNIFORM MARRIAGE AND DIVORCE ACT (1970)
PART IV—CUSTODY

The following is reprinted from Part IV of the above act which has been adopted in about ten states.

Section 401. Commencement of Proceeding, Jurisdiction

(a) [If a court of this state has jurisdiction pursuant to the Uniform Child Custody Jurisdiction Act,] a child custody proceeding is commenced in the [   ] court:

(1) by a parent
    (i) by filing a petition for dissolution or legal separation; or
    (ii) by filing a petition seeking custody of the child in the [county, judicial district] where the child is permanently resident or where he is found; or

(2) by a person other than a parent, by filing a petition seeking custody of the child in the [county, judicial district] where the child is permanently resident or where he is found, but only if the child is not in the physical custody of one of its parents. . . .

Section 402. Best Interests of Child The court shall determine custody in accordance with the best interests of the child. The court shall consider all relevant factors including:

(1) the wishes of the child's parent or parents as to his custody;

943

(2) the wishes of the child as to his custodian;

(3) the interaction and interrelationship of the child with his parent or parents, his siblings, and any other person who may significantly affect the child's best interests;

(4) the child's adjustment to his home, school, and community; and

(5) the mental and physical health of all individuals involved.

The court shall not consider conduct of a proposed custodian that does not affect his relationship to the child. . . .

Section 404. Interviews

(2) The court may interview the child in chambers to ascertain the child's wishes as to his custodian. The court may permit counsel to be present at the interview. The court shall cause a record of the interview to be made and to be made part of the record in the case.

(b) The court may seek the advice of professional personnel whether or not they are employed on a regular basis by the court. The advice given shall be in writing and shall be made available by the court to counsel upon request. Counsel may call for cross-examination any professional personnel consulted by the court.

Section 405. Investigations and Reports

(a) In contested custody proceedings, and in other custody proceedings if a parent or the child's custodian so requests, the court may order an investigation and report concerning custodial arrangements for the child. The investigation and report may be made by [the court social service agency, the staff of the juvenile court, the local probation or welfare department, or a private agency employed by the court for the purpose].

(b) In preparing his report concerning a child, the investigator may consult any person who may have information about the child and his potential custodial arrangements. Upon order of the court, the investigator may refer the child to professional personnel for diagnosis. The investigator may consult with and obtain information from medical, psychiatric, or other expert persons who have served the child in the past without obtaining the consent of the parent or the child's custodian; but the child's consent must be obtained if he has reached the age of 16, unless the court finds that he lacks mental capacity to consent. If the requirements of subsection (c) are fulfilled, the investigator's report may be received in evidence at the hearing.

(c) The court shall mail the investigator's report to counsel and to any party not represented by counsel at least 10 days prior to the hearing. The investigator shall make available to counsel and to any party not represented by counsel the investigator's file of underlying data and reports, complete texts of diagnostic reports made to the investigator pursuant to the provisions of subsection (b), and the names and addresses of all persons whom the investigator has consulted. Any party to the proceeding may call the investigator and any person whom he has consulted for cross-examination. A party may not waive his right of cross-examination prior to the hearing. . . .

Section 407. Visitation

(a) A parent not granted custody of the child is entitled to reasonable visitation rights unless the court finds, after a hearing, that visitation would endanger the child's physical health or significantly impair his emotional development.

(b) The court may modify an order granting or denying visitation rights whenever modification would serve the best interests of the child; but the court shall not restrict a parent's visitation rights unless it finds that the visitation would endanger the child's physical health or significantly impair his emotional development. . . .

Section 409. Modification

(a) No motion to modify a custody decree may be made earlier than one year after the date of the initial decree. If a motion for modification has been filed, whether or not it was granted, no subsequent motion may be filed within 2 years after disposition of the prior motion, unless the court decides . . . that there is reason to believe that the child's present environment may endanger his physical health or significantly impair his emotional development.

(b) [If a court of this state has jurisdiction pursuant to the Uniform Child Custody Jurisdiction Act,] the court shall not modify a prior custody decree unless it finds, upon the basis of facts that have arisen since the prior decree or that were unknown to the court at the time of the prior decree, that a change has occurred in the circumstances of the child or his custodian and that the modification is necessary to serve the best interests of the child. In applying these standards the court shall retain the custodian established by the prior decree unless:

(1) the custodian agrees to the modification;

(2) the child has been integrated into the family of the petitioner with the consent of the custodian; or

(3) the child's present environment endangers his physical health or significantly impairs his emotional development and the harm likely to be caused by a change of environment is outweighed by the advantage of a change to the child. . . .

B

UNIFORM CHILD CUSTODY JURISDICTION ACT

The following is taken from New York Domestic Relations Law, Article 5-A, which was added by Laws 1977, Ch. 493, eff. Sept. 1, 1978.

Summary of Article

---

§ 75-b.   **Purposes of article; construction of provisions.**

1. The general purposes of this article are to:

(a) avoid jurisdictional competition and conflict with courts of other states in matters of child custody which have in the past resulted in the shifting of children from state to state with harmful effects on their well-being.

(b) promote cooperation with the courts of other states to the end that a custody decree is rendered in that state which can best decide the case in the interest of the child;

(c) assure that litigation concerning the custody of a child take place ordinarily in the state with which the child and his family have the closest connection and where significant evidence concerning his care, protection, training, and personal relationships is most readily available, and that courts of this state decline the exercise of jurisdiction when the child and his family have closer connection with another state;

(d) discourage continuing controversies over child custody in the interest of greater stability of home environment and of secure family relationships for the child;

(e) deter abductions and other unilateral removals of children undertaken to obtain custody awards;

(f) avoid re-litigation of custody decisions of other states in this state insofar as feasible;

(g) facilitate the enforcement of custody decrees of other states;

(h) promote and expand the exchange of information and other forms of mutual assistance between the courts of this state and those of other states concerned with the same child; and

(i) make uniform the law of those states which enact it.

2. This article shall be construed to promote the general purposes stated in this section.

§ 75-c. Definitions.

As used in this article, the following terms have the following meanings:

1. "Contestant" means a person, including a parent, who claims a right to custody or visitation rights with respect to a child.

2. "Custody determination" means a court decision and court orders and instructions providing for the temporary or permanent custody of a child, including visitation rights.

3. "Custody proceeding" includes proceedings in which a custody determination is at issue or is one of several issues including any action or proceeding brought to annul a marriage or to declare the nullity of a void marriage, or for a separation, or for a divorce, but not including proceedings for adoption, child protective proceedings or proceedings for permanent termination of parental custody, or pro-

ceedings involving the guardianship and custody of neglected or dependent children, or proceedings initiated pursuant to section three hundred fifty-eight-a of the social services law.

4. "Decree" or "custody decree" means a custody determination contained in a judicial decree or order made in a custody proceeding, and includes an initial decree and a modification decree.

5. "Home state" means the state in which the child at the time of the commencement of the custody proceeding, has resided with his parents, a parent, or a person acting as parent, for at least six consecutive months. In the case of a child less than six months old at the time of the commencement of the proceeding, home state means the state in which the child has resided with any of such persons for a majority of the time since birth.

6. "Initial decree" means the first custody decree concerning a particular child.

7. "Modification decree" means a custody decree which modifies or replaces a prior decree, whether made by the court which rendered the prior decree or by another court.

8. "Physical custody" means actual possession and control of a child.

9. "Person acting as parent" means a person, other than a parent, who has physical custody of a child and who has either been awarded custody by a court or claims a right to custody.

10. "State" means any state, territory, or possession of the United States, the Commonwealth of Puerto Rico, and the District of Columbia.

§ 75-d. Jurisdiction to make child custody determinations.

1. A court of this state which is competent to decide child custody matters has jurisdiction to make a child custody determination by initial or modification decree only when:

(a) this state (i) is the home state of the child at the time of commencement of the custody proceeding, or (ii) had been the child's home state within six months before commencement of such proceeding and the child is absent from this state because of his removal or retention by a person claiming his custody or for other reasons, and a parent or person acting as parent continues to live in this state; or

(b) it is in the best interest of the child that a court of this state assume jurisdiction because (i) the child and his parents, or the child and at least one contestant, have a significant connection with this state, and (ii) there is within the jurisdiction of the court substantial evidence concerning the child's present or future care, protection, training, and personal relationships; or

(c) the child is physically present in this state and (i) the child has been abandoned or (ii) it is necessary in any emergency to protect the child; or

(d) (i) it appears that no other state would have jurisdiction under prerequisites substantially in accordance with paragraph (a), (b), or (c), or another state has declined to exercise jurisdiction on the ground that this state is the more appropriate forum to determine the custody of the child, and (ii) it is in the best interest of the child that this court assume jurisdiction.

2. Except under paragraphs (c) and (d) of subdivision one of this section, physical presence in this state of the child, or of the child and one of the contestants, is not alone sufficient to confer jurisdiction on a court of this state to make a child custody determination.

3. Physical presence of the child, while desirable, is not a prerequisite for jurisdiction to determine his custody.

§ 75-e. Notice and opportunity to be heard.

Before making a decree under this article, reasonable notice and opportunity to be heard shall be given to the contestants, any parent whose parental rights have not been previously terminated, and any person who has physical custody of the child. If any of these persons is outside the state, notice and opportunity to be heard shall be given pursuant to section seventy-five-f of this article. Any person who is given notice and an opportunity to be heard pursuant to this section shall be deemed a party to the proceeding for all purposes under this article.

§ 75-f. Notice to persons outside the state.

1. If a person cannot be personally served with notice within the state, the court shall require that such person be served in a manner reasonably calculated to give actual notice, as follows:

(a) by personal delivery outside the state in the manner prescribed in section three hundred thirteen of the civil practice law and rules;

(b) by any form of mail addressed to the person and requesting a receipt; or

(c) in such manner as the court, upon motion, directs, including publication, if service is impracticable under paragraph (a) or (b) of subdivision one of this section.

2. Notice under this section shall be served, mailed, delivered, or last published at least twenty days before any hearing in this state.

3. Proof of service outside the state shall be by affidavit of the individual who made the service, or in the manner prescribed by the order pursuant to which the service is made. If service is made by mail, proof may be a receipt signed by the addressee or other evidence of delivery to the addressee.

4. Notice is not required if a person submits to the jurisdiction of the court.

§ 75-g. Simultaneous proceedings in other states.

1. A court of this state shall not exercise its jurisdiction under this article if at the time of filing the petition a proceeding concerning the custody of the child was pending in a court of another state exercising jurisdiction substantially in conformity with this article, unless the proceeding is stayed by the court of the other state because this state is a more appropriate forum or for other reasons.

2. Before hearing the petition in a custody proceeding the court shall examine the pleadings and other information supplied by the

parties under section seventy-five-j of this article. If the court has reason to believe that proceedings may be pending in another state it shall direct an inquiry to the state court administrator or other appropriate official of the other state.

3. If the court is informed during the course of the proceeding that a proceeding concerning the custody of the child was pending in another state before the court assumed jurisdiction it shall stay the proceeding and communicate with the court in which the other proceeding is pending to the end that the issue may be litigated in the more appropriate forum and that information be exchanged in accordance with sections seventy-five-s through seventy-five-v of this article. If a court of this state has made a custody decree before being informed of a pending proceeding in a court of another state, it shall immediately inform that court of the fact. If the court is informed that a proceeding was commenced in another state after it assumed jurisdiction, it shall likewise inform the other court to the end that the issues may be litigated in the more appropriate forum.

§ 75-h.   Inconvenient forum.

1. A court which has jurisdiction under this article to make an initial or modification decree may decline to exercise its jurisdiction any time before making a decree if it finds that it is an inconvenient forum to make a custody determination under the circumstances of the case and that a court of another state is a more appropriate forum.

2. A finding of inconvenient forum may be made upon the court's own motion or upon motion of a party or a guardian ad litem or other representative of the child.

3. In determining if it is an inconvenient forum, the court shall consider if it is in the interest of the child that another state assume jurisdiction. For this purpose it may take into account the following factors, among others, whether:

(a) another state is or recently was the child's home state;

(b) another state has a closer connection with the child and his family or with the child and one or more of the contestants;

(c) substantial evidence concerning the child's present or future care, protection, training, and personal relationships is more readily available in another state;

(d) the parties have agreed on another forum which is no less appropriate; and

(e) the exercise of jurisdiction by a court of this state would contravene any of the purposes stated in section seventy-five-b of this article.

4. Before determining whether to decline or retain jurisdiction the court may communicate with a court of another state and exchange information pertinent to the assumption of jurisdiction by either court with a view to assuring that jurisdiction will be exercised by the more appropriate court and that a forum will be available to the parties.

5. If the court finds that it is an inconvenient forum and that a court of another state is a more appropriate forum, it may dismiss the proceedings, or it may stay the proceedings upon condition that a custody proceeding be promptly commenced in another named state or upon any other conditions which may be just and proper, including the condition that a moving party stipulate his consent and submission to the jurisdiction of the other forum.

6. Where the court has jurisdiction of an action or proceeding brought to annul a marriage or to declare the nullity of a void marriage or for a separation or for a divorce, the court may decline to exercise jurisdiction of an application for a custody determination made therein while retaining jurisdiction of the matrimonial action.

7. If it appears to the court that it is clearly an inappropriate forum it may require the party who commenced the proceedings to pay, in addition to the costs of the proceedings in this state, necessary travel and other expenses, including attorneys' fees, incurred by other parties or their witnesses. Payment shall be made to the clerk of the court for remittance to the proper party.

8. Upon dismissal or stay of proceedings under this section the court shall inform the court found to be the more appropriate forum of such dismissal or stay, or if the court which would have jurisdic-

tion in the other state is not certainly known, shall transmit the information to the court administrator or other appropriate official for forwarding to the appropriate court.

9. Any communication received from another state to the effect that its courts have made a finding of inconvenient forum because a court of this state is the more appropriate forum shall be filed with the clerk of the appropriate court. Upon assuming jurisdiction the court of this state shall inform the original court of this fact.

§ 75-i.   Jurisdiction declined because of conduct.

1. If the petitioner for an initial decree has wrongfully taken the child from another state or has engaged in similar reprehensible conduct the court may decline to exercise jurisdiction if this is just and proper under the circumstances.

2. Unless required in the interest of the child, the court shall not exercise its jurisdiction to modify a custody decree of another state if the petitioner, without consent of the person entitled to custody, has improperly removed the child from the physical custody of the person entitled to custody or has improperly retained the child after a visit or other temporary relinquishment of physical custody. If the petitioner has violated any other provision of a custody decree of another state the court may decline to exercise its jurisdiction if this is just and proper under the circumstances.

3. In appropriate cases a court dismissing a petition under this section may charge the petitioner with necessary travel and other expenses, including attorneys' fees, incurred by other parties or their witnesses.

§ 75-j.   Pleadings and affidavits; duty to inform court.

1. Except as provided in subdivision four of this section, every party to a custody proceeding shall, in his first pleading or in an affidavit attached to that pleading, give information under oath as to the child's present address, the places where the child has lived within the last five years, and the names and present addresses of the persons

with whom the child has lived during that period. In this pleading or affidavit every party shall further declare under oath whether he:

(a) has participated as a party, witness, or in any other capacity in any other litigation concerning the custody of the same child in this or any other state;

(b) has information of any custody proceeding concerning the child pending in a court of this or any other state; and

(c) knows of any person not a party to the proceedings who has physical custody of the child or claims to have custody or visitation rights with respect to the child.

2. If the declaration as to any of the above items is in the affirmative the declarant shall give additional information under oath as required by the court. The court may examine the parties under oath as to details of the information furnished and as to other matters pertinent to the court's jurisdiction and the disposition of the case.

3. If, during the pendency of a custody proceeding, any party learns of another custody proceeding concerning the child in this or another state, he shall immediately inform the court of this fact.

4. In an action for divorce or separation, or to annul a marriage or declare the nullity of a void marriage, where neither party is in default in appearance of pleading and the issue of custody is uncontested, the affidavit required by this section need not be submitted. In any other such action, such affidavit shall be submitted by the parties within twenty days after joinder of issue on the question of custody, or at the time application for a default judgment is made.

§ 75-k.   Additional parties.

If the court learns from information furnished by the parties pursuant to section seventy-five-j of this article, or from other sources that a person not a party to the custody proceeding has physical custody of the child or claims to have custody or visitation rights with respect to the child, it shall order that person to be joined as a party and to be duly notified of the pendency of the proceeding and of his joinder as a party. If the person joined as a party is outside this state he shall be served with process or otherwise notified in accordance with section seventy-five-f of this article.

§ 75-l. Appearance of parties and the child.

1. The court may order any party to the proceeding who is in the state to appear personally before the court. If that party has physical custody of the child the court may order that he appear personally with the child.

2. If a party to the proceeding whose presence is desired by the court is outside the state with or without the child the court may order that the notice given under section seventy-five-f of this article include a statement directing that party to appear personally with or without the child and declaring that failure to appear may result in a decision adverse to that party.

3. If a party to the proceeding who is outside the state is directed to appear under subdivision two or desires to appear personally before the court with or without the child, the court may require another party to pay to the clerk of the court travel and other necessary expenses of the party so appearing and of the child if this is just and proper under the circumstances.

§ 75-m. Force and effect of custody decrees.

A custody decree rendered by a court of this state which had jurisdiction under section seventy-five-d of this article shall be binding upon all parties who have been personally served in this state or notified pursuant to section seventy-five-f of this article or who have submitted to the jurisdiction of the court, and who have been given an opportunity to be heard. As to these parties the custody decree is conclusive as to all issues of law and fact decided and as to the custody determination made unless and until that determination is modified pursuant to law, including the provisions of this article.

§ 75-n. Recognition of out-of-state custody decrees.

The courts of this state shall recognize and enforce an initial or modification decree of a court of another state which had assumed jurisdiction under statutory provisions substantially in accordance with this article or which was made under factual circumstances meeting the jurisdictional standards of this article, so long as the decree has not been modified in accordance with jurisdictional standards substantially similar to those of this article.

§ 75-o. Modification of custody of decree of another state.

1. If a court of another state has made a custody decree, a court of this state shall not modify that decree unless (1) it appears to the court of this state that the court which rendered the decree does not now have jurisdiction under jurisdictional prerequisites substantially in accordance with this article or has declined to assume jurisdiction to modify the decree and (2) the court of this state has jurisdiction.

2. If a court of this state is authorized under subdivision one of this section and section seventy-five-i of this article to modify a custody decree of another state, it shall give due consideration to the transcript of the record and other documents of all previous proceedings submitted to it in accordance with section seventy-five-v of this article.

§ 75-p. Filing and enforcement of custody decree of another state.

1. A certified copy of a custody decree of another state may be filed in the office of the clerk of the supreme court or of the family court. The clerk shall treat the decree in the same manner as a custody decree of the supreme court or of the family court. A custody decree so filed has the same effect and shall be enforced in like manner as a custody decree rendered by a court of this state.

2. A person violating a custody decree of another state which makes it necessary to enforce the decree in this state may be required to pay necessary travel and other expenses, including attorneys' fees, incurred by the party entitled to the custody or his witnesses.

§ 75-q. Certified copies of custody decrees.

The clerk of the supreme court or the family court, at the request of the court of another state or, upon payment of the appropriate fees, if any, at the request of a party to the custody proceeding, the attorney for a party or a representative of the child shall certify and forward a copy of the decree to that court or person.

§ 75-r.   Examination of witnesses outside the state.

In addition to other procedural devices available to a party, any party to the proceeding or a guardian ad litem or other representative of the child may examine witnesses, including parties and the child, in another state by deposition or otherwise in accordance with the applicable provisions of the civil practice law and rules.

§ 75-s.   Hearings and studies in another state; orders to appear.

1. A court of this state may request the appropriate court of another state to hold a hearing to adduce evidence, to order a party within its jurisdiction, to produce or give evidence under other procedures of that state, or to have social studies made with respect to the custody of a child involved in proceedings pending in the court of this state; and to forward to the court of this state certified copies of the transcript of the record of the hearing, the evidence otherwise adduced, or any social studies prepared in compliance with the request. The cost of the services may be assessed against the parties.

2. A court of this state may request the appropriate court of another state to order a party to custody proceedings pending in the court of this state to appear in the proceedings, and if that party has physical custody of the child, to appear with the child. The request may state that travel and other necessary expenses of the party and of the child whose appearance is desired will be assessed against another party or will otherwise be paid.

§ 75-t.   Assistance to courts of other states.

1. Upon request of the court of another state the courts of this state which are competent to hear custody matters may order a party or witness in this state to appear at an examination to be conducted in the same manner as if such person were a party to or witness in an action pending in the supreme court. A certified copy of the deposi-

tion or the evidence otherwise adduced shall be forwarded by the clerk of the court to the court which requested it.

2. A person within the state may voluntarily give his testimony or statement for use in a custody proceeding outside this state.

3. Upon request of the court of another state a competent court of this state may order a person within the state to appear alone or with the child in a custody proceeding in another state. The court may condition compliance with the request upon assurance by the other state that travel and other necessary expenses will be advanced or reimbursed.

§ 75-u. Preservation of evidence for use in other states.

In any custody proceeding in this state the court shall preserve the pleadings, orders and decrees, any record that has been made of its hearings, social studies, and other pertinent documents until the child reaches twenty-one years of age. Upon appropriate request of the court of another state the court shall forward to the other court certified copies of any or all of such documents.

§ 75-v. Request for court records from another state.

If a custody decree has been rendered in another state concerning a child involved in a custody proceeding pending in a court of this state, the court of this state upon taking jurisdiction of the case shall request of the court of the other state a certified copy of the transcript of any court record and other documents mentioned in section seventy-five-u.

§ 75-w. International application.

The general policies of this article extend to the international area. The provisions of this article relating to the recognition and enforcement of custody decrees of other states apply to custody decrees and decrees involving legal institutions similar in nature to custody institutions rendered by appropriate authorities of other nations if reasonable notice and opportunity to be heard were given to all affected persons.

§ 75-x. Priority.

Upon the request of a party to a custody proceeding which raises a question of existence or exercise of jurisdiction under this article the case shall be given calendar priority and handled expeditiously.

§ 75-y. Separability.

If any part of this article or the application thereof to any person or circumstances is adjudged invalid by a court of competent jurisdiction, such judgment shall not affect or impair the validity of the remainder of such article or the application thereof to other persons and circumstances.

§ 75-z. Inconsistent provisions of other laws superseded.

Insofar as the provisions of this article are inconsistent with the provisions of any other law, general, special or local, the provisions of this article shall be controlling.

C

MICHIGAN CHILD CUSTODY ACT OF 1970

The following is reprinted from Mich. Comp. Laws Ann.
§§ 722.22-722-27 (Supp. 1971):

722.23   Best interests of the child, definition. "Best interests of the
child" means the sum total of the following factors to be considered,
evaluated and determined by the court:

(a) The love, affection and other emotional ties existing between
the competing parties and the child.

(b) The capacity and disposition of competing parties to give the
child love, affection and guidance and continuation of educating and
raising of the child in its religion or creed, if any.

(c) The capacity and disposition of competing parties to provide
the child with food, clothing, medical care or other remedial care
recognized and permitted under the laws of this state in lieu of
medical care, and other material needs.

(d) The length of time the child has lived in a stable, satisfactory
environment and the desirability of maintaining continuity.

(e) The permanence, as a family unit, of the existing or proposed
custodial home.

(f) The moral fitness of the competing parties.

(g) The mental and physical health of the competing parties.

(h) The home, school and community record of the child.

(i) The reasonable preference of the child, if the court deems the child to be of sufficient age to express preference.

(j) Any other factor considered by the court to be relevant to a particular child custody dispute.

722.24   Child's inherent rights, declaration; custody, support, and visitation, establishment. In all actions now pending or hereafter filed in a circuit court involving dispute of custody of a minor child, the court shall declare the inherent rights of the child and establish the rights and duties as to custody, support and visitation of the child in accordance with this act.

722.25   Best interests of the child, effect, presumption. When the dispute is between the parents, between agencies or between third persons the best interests of the child shall control. When the dispute is between the parent or parents and an agency or a third person, it is presumed that the best interests of the child are served by awarding custody to the parent or parents, unless the contrary is established by clear and convincing evidence.

722.26   Liberal construction; application.... The provisions of this act, being equitable in nature, shall be liberally construed and applied to establish promptly the rights of the child and the rights and duties of the parties involved. This act shall apply to all circuit court child custody disputes and actions, whether original or incidental to other actions. . . .

722.27   Custody, support, and visitation; awards, judgments, orders; modifications, amendments; community resources; guardian ad litem; counsel. If a child custody dispute has been submitted to a circuit court as an original action under this act or has arisen incidentally from other actions therein or orders or judgments thereof, for the best interests of the child the court may:

(a) Award the custody of the child to any of the parties involved or to others and provide for payment of support for the child, until the child reaches the age of 18 years or in exceptional circumstances, until the child reaches majority. . . .

(c) Modify or amend its previous judgments or orders for proper cause shown or because of change of circumstances until the child reaches the age of 18 years or in exceptional circumstances, until the child reaches majority. The court shall not modify or amend its previous judgments or orders or issue a new order so as to change the established custodial environment of a child unless there is presented clear and convincing evidence that it is in the best interest of the child. The custodial environment of a child is established if over an appreciable time the child naturally looks to the custodian in such environment for guidance, discipline, the necessities of life and parental comfort. The age of the child, the physical environment and the inclination of the custodian and the child as to permanency of the relationship shall also be considered.

(d) Utilize the community resources in behavioral sciences and other professions in the investigation and study of custody disputes and consider their recommendations for the resolution of the disputes.

(e) Appoint a guardian ad litem or counsel for the child and assess the costs and reasonable fees against any or all parties involved, totally or partially.

(f) Take any other action considered to be necessary in a particular child custody dispute.

D

THE BILL OF RIGHTS OF CHILDREN IN DIVORCE ACTIONS

The following has been adapted by The Family Court of Milwaukee County from recent decisions of the Wisconsin Supreme Court

---

I. The right to be treated as an interested and affected person and not as a pawn, possession or chattel of either or both parents.

II. The right to grow to maturity in that home environment which will best guarantee an opportunity for the child to grow to mature and responsible citizenship.

III. The right to the day by day love, care, discipline and protection of the parent having custody of the child.

IV. The right to know the non-custodial parent and to have the benefit of such parent's love and guidance through adequate visitations.

V. The right to a positive and constructive relationship with both parents, with neither parent to be permitted to degrade or downgrade the other in the mind of the child.

VI. The right to have moral and ethical values developed by precept and practices and to have limits set for behavior so that the child early in life may develop self-discipline and self-control.

VII. The right to the most adequate level of economic support that can be provided by the best efforts of both parents.

VIII. The right to the same opportunities for education that the child would have if the family unit had not been broken.

IX. The right to periodic review of custodial arrangements and child support orders as the circumstances of the parents and the benefit of the child may require.

X. The right to recognition that children involved in a divorce are always disadvantaged parties and that the law must take affirmative steps to protect their welfare, including, where indicated, a social investigation to determine, and the appointment of a guardian ad litem to protect their interests.

ACKNOWLEDGMENTS TO CONTRIBUTORS

The program of the Group for the Advancement of Psychiatry, a nonprofit, tax exempt organization, is made possible largely through the voluntary contributions and efforts of its members. For their financial assistance during the past fiscal year in helping it to fulfill its aims, GAP is grateful to the following:

American Charitable Foundation
Dr. and Mrs. Jeffrey Aron
Dr. and Mrs. Richard Aron
Virginia & Nathan Bederman Foundation
Maurice Falk Medical Fund
Geigy Pharmaceuticals
Mrs. Carol Gold
The Gralnick Foundation
The Grove Foundation
The Holzheimer Fund
Ittleson Foundation, Inc., for the Blanche F. Ittleson Consultation Program
McNeil Laboratories
Merck, Sharp & Dohme Laboratories
Merrell—National Laboratories
Phillips Foundation
Sandoz Pharmaceuticals
The Murray L. Silberstein Fund (Mrs. Allan H. Kalmus)
Smith Kline & French Laboratories
Mr. and Mrs. Herman Spertus
E.R. Squibb & Sons, Inc.
Jerome Stone Family Foundation
van Ameringen Foundation
Mr. S. Winn
Wyeth Laboratories

OTHER RECENT PUBLICATIONS
GROUP FOR THE ADVANCEMENT OF PSYCHIATRY

Orders amounting to less than $10.00 must be accompanied by remittance. All prices are subject to change without notice.

GAP publications may be ordered on a subscription basis. The current subscription cycle comprising the Volume X Series covers the period from July 1, 1977 to June 30, 1980. For further information, write the Publications Office (see below).

Bound volumes of GAP publications issued since 1947 are also available which include GAP titles no longer in print and no longer available in any other form. A bound index of volumes (I through VII) has been published separately.

Please send your order and remittance to: Publications Office, Mental Health Materials Center, 30 East 29th Street, New York, New York 10016.